Build
Green
and Save

Build Green and Save

Protecting the Earth and Your Bottom Line

Matt Belcher

BuilderBooks.com®
BOOKS THAT BUILD YOUR BUSINESS

A Service of
NAHB
NATIONAL ASSOCIATION
OF HOME BUILDERS

Build Green & Save: Protecting the Earth and Your Bottom Line

BuilderBooks, a Service of the National Association of Home Builders

Courtenay S. Brown	Director, Book Publishing & Editor
Natalie C. Holmes	Book Editor
Torrie L. Singletary	Production Editor
Design Central, Inc.	Cover Design
Circle Graphics	Composition
District Creative Printing Inc.	Printing
Gerald M. Howard	NAHB Executive Vice President and CEO
Mark Pursell	NAHB Senior Vice President, Exhibitions, Marketing & Sales Group
Lakisha Campbell	NAHB Vice President, Publishing & Affinity Programs

Printed in the United States of America

12 11 10 09   1 2 3 4 5

ISBN -10: 0-86718-644-5
ISBN-13: 978-0-86718-644-4

Library of Congress Cataloging-in-Publication Data

Belcher, Matt.
  Build green & save : protecting the Earth and your bottom line / Matt Belcher.
    p. cm.
  ISBN-13: 978-0-86718-644-4
  ISBN-10: 0-86718-644-5
  1. Sustainable buildings--Design and construction. 2. Environmental protection--Citizen participation. 3. Building--Cost control. I. Title. II. Title: Build green and save.

  TH880.B45 2009
  690'.8047--dc22

                                                                                    2009012633

For further information, please contact:

National Association of Home Builders
1201 15th Street, NW
Washington, DC 20005-2800
800-223-2665
Visit us online at www.BuilderBooks.com.

CONTENTS

List of Figures

ACKNOWLEDGMENTS

I want to thank everyone I have learned from and those who have befriended and helped me along the way. In addition to those who are mentioned throughout this book, I thank Ray Tonjes, Eric Borsting, and my fellow Green Building and Energy Committee members and staff.

I also thank my colleagues in St. Louis, especially my competitors. (We actually refer to our working relationship as *co-opetition*—we work together to raise the level of our service to our customers, so that all of our bottom lines rise together.)

I explicitly thank Patrick Sullivan, executive vice president of the Home Builder's Association of St. Louis and Eastern Missouri. I sat next to Patrick on a flight to the National Association of Home Builders

(NAHB) Fall Board meetings a few years ago. He wanted to start a green building program and asked if I would chair it. Everyone who knows Patrick also knows when he thinks enough of you to do something for him, the last thing you want to do is let him down.

I acknowledge David S. Jaffe, Vice President, NAHB Legal Affairs, an expert at advising builders on managing risks with regards to green building. (If you get the chance to catch David's presentation at the NAHB Green Building Conference, it is worth the price of admission. It can actually save you a lot of time and money down the road. Be sure to tell David I sent you!)

I also thank my good friend and counsel, Scott Dickenson of Lathrop-Gage, who has helped shape some of my business practices.

And most importantly, I thank my wife and daughters. Being a builder isn't always easy. Being the wife of a builder is just plain tough!

ABOUT THE AUTHOR

Matt Belcher is a builder, developer and nationally-recognized green building consultant. He has been actively involved in the St. Louis area construction industry for 30 years, 6 of which he spent as a top building codes official in the St. Louis region.

In 1993, he founded Belcher Homes, an award-winning company that specializes in constructing sustainable green homes and light commercial construction using low-impact, ecological development. Belcher Homes is committed to the "whole building" design approach, a philosophy that every decision in the context of its immediate or eventual impact will have on the ecosystem. Belcher Homes is a partner with the University of Missouri's Institute of Environmental and Energy Technologies (ENTECH), which promotes training and business stimulation and research in green building, development and energy efficient practices.

Mr. Belcher has also lent his expertise to lobbying efforts for green building legislation and has advised others on managing legal risks associated with green building as a member of the Construction Dispute Resolution Services National Panel of Green Construction Specialists. He also assists home builder associations (HBAs) in developing green building programs and promoting green building practices.

Mr. Belcher serves on the Board of Directors of the NAHB and NAHB's Green Building and Energy subcommittees. He also serves on the Board of Directors of the Green Building Initiative. He chaired NAHB's National Green Building Conference in 2006 and 2007.

In 2007, he served as president of the HBA of St. Louis and Eastern Missouri. He has also served on the HBA's Building Codes committee for 15 years, including 7 years as its chairman. Mr. Belcher helped organize the St. Louis HBA's green building effort and has served as its chair for the past three years. He is also a member of the St. Louis Chapter of the U.S. Green Building Council.

In 2008, Mr. Belcher testified on behalf of the NAHB before the U.S. House Energy and Air Quality Subcommittee on climate benefits of improved building energy efficiency.

To learn more about Belcher Homes, visit www.belcherhomes.com

INTRODUCTION

Why build green?

They say the apple doesn't fall far from the tree, and I'm living proof: I grew up in the building industry, and I learned the general idea and philosophy of building green from my dad. Long before climate concerns and clean and efficient energy spawned the current movement, my dad built green—without even realizing it. He was in the lumber business, and as far as he was concerned his methods were just common sense; they saved him money and made his customers happy. His methods have always made sense to me, too. My dad built homes that were sustainable and livable. I can't imagine building any other way; that's why I build green.

The facts speak for themselves—according to the U.S. Census Bureau the U.S. population topped 300 million in March 2009. Worldwide, approximately 10,000 babies are born every hour, adding to the world's current population of about 6.5 billion by leaps and bounds. All of these people need a place to live.

Yet, our planet is not getting any bigger, and natural resources do not perpetually renew themselves, especially not at the same rate at which we consume them. As the population continues to grow, nature and its bounty are becoming scarcer and thus more valuable. Creating shelter for a rapidly expanding population will put a strain on natural resources, so we must use them wisely.

As home builders, our job is to provide shelter and respond to the demand for housing. When we construct new dwellings and rehab existing homes, we have the power to decide how to best use our natural resources. We can conserve these precious resources, or we can pretend they are infinite and waste them with no thought of future consequences. If we view our natural resources as the commodities they are and begin to understand that their value increases as they become more scarce, then, as with any commodity investment, we would want to maximize its efficiency to produce a greater return on investment—that is, financial investment and investment in our future.

Essentially our work is embedded in the environment. Therefore, it is not that difficult to implement the use of materials that are recyclable, renewable, and reusable. Green builders view the house, the site and the surrounding environment as interlocking groups of systems that require careful planning and management.

Although homes built today are 100% more energy efficient than those built 10 years ago, we have a unique opportunity to lessen our impact on the environment even further. In the following chapters I will share my tried-and-true green building experiences and provide insight into how Belcher Homes plans and constructs homes that are practical, sustainable, and most importantly, affordable.

> When we consume, we must reuse, renew and recycle. In a word, we must become more efficient.

Why build green? It's simple. Green housing is healthier to occupy, due to its materials, components, and construction methods. A healthy house can lower residents' health care expenses and provide a superior quality of life. Furthermore, ongoing maintenance and operating expenses in green homes are lower than those incurred in nongreen housing. Therefore, if you total the monthly mortgage payment, utility payment, and maintenance costs, the aggregate amount spent living in a green home is lower than in a traditional home. Sometimes, the cost can be dramatically lower.

Emerging competition in green manufacturing has increased the number of green materials available at lower prices, benefiting both builders and consumers. In fact, green manufacturing has become the largest manufacturing segment of the U.S. economy. Even nongreen builders are probably building greener than they realize, because of changes in the materials they use and in building code requirements. This all adds up to making green construction more affordable.

Why build green? Building green raises the bar for the housing industry as a whole by establishing new standards for durability, livability, and sustainability. Building green is building smart.

CHAPTER 1

THE BUSINESS OF BUILDING GREEN

I often tell my clients "I love what I do but my wife insists I make money at it!" It is rewarding to be in an industry that is revolutionizing its business practices to be more green. I have always been committed to doing the right thing the right way. But as builders and consumers explore implications of making their homes greener, we must remember that economics also shape—and benefit from—our industry. This fact cannot be overlooked as we incorporate green practices. Company size will determine the effect that incorporating green building has on a builder's business, as consumer demand for green building grows and builders respond to that demand.

So far, the green building market has emerged and green building has spread mainly through small and custom building firms. These firms are accustomed to being more adaptable. They are used to pricing jobs individually as part of their normal business practices. These builders also help determine to a significant degree the overall economics of the building industry. They have proven the theories of green building and the impact it could have on the industry.

Conversely, production builders' business plans are based on cost efficiency and expeditiousness in the building process, which allows the residential construction industry to be viable. In most cases, production builders' costs and time lines are precise. Their construction plans rely on predictable costs and set schedules.

If green building enables smaller volume builders to build more efficiently, larger volume builders should be able to reap exponentially greater benefits since their business model depends to a greater extent on production efficiency.

In an October 2008 report, *The Green Home Builder: Navigating for Success in a Down Economy*, McGraw-Hill Construction revisited NAHB's first examination into green building in the residential sector in 2006. Their research indicated that green building is still trending upward. Forty percent of builders surveyed in the report stated that green makes it easier for them to market their homes.

The results further show that by the end of 2008, 6–10% of the market ($12–$20 billion) would be green compared to 2% ($7 billion) two years ago. By far the largest reason builders gave for going green was "quality" and "doing the right thing." It seems to be paying off as these builders begin to serve a more discriminating clientele.

Cost has been one of the biggest obstacles to building green, but with manufacturers of building components shifting their focus to green, the cost gap is closing significantly. There are also other ancillary costs that are positively affected such as increased equity in these homes and cost savings to the builder as a result of waste reduction and more efficient use of materials. As a result, it will not be long before green building is simply the norm.

Beware of Greenwashing

As recently as just a few years ago, we would spend a considerable amount of time researching material safety data sheets (MSDS) to verify the contents of the materials we were using to build our homes. Now manufacturers are tapping into the green market, thereby making product verification much easier for builders. Product vendors have learned that if they want to sell to green builders, they must fabricate components that improve home building efficiency. Many have been able to do this and maintain their bottom line. However, builders must be diligent and investigate salespeople's casual claims about their product's attributes.

For example, some manufacturers do not understand the specific information you need or what effect their component or materials may have on a home's indoor air quality. Then there's *greenwashing,* or inflated advertising claims about a product to appeal to consumers seeking green homes. Product claims about green materials, without objective data to prove them, can be a legal liability in selling to consumers.

Green choices equal efficient choices. As everyone goes green, products and processes should become more efficient and prices more competitive.

Set Realistic Expectations

As with any construction project, setting expectations and documenting that the prospective home buyer understands the expectations is key. Most prospective clients have some idea of what green building means, but few know how all encompassing it is or for that matter, what *green* means. When we meet with prospective clients, we listen carefully to their ideas about green building. Then, we educate them about what green really means.

We explain that the term *green* is a general term for a type of housing similar to the terms *active adult* or *universal design.* We carefully explain that the home will be constructed in accordance with the plans, specifications, and contract. We do not make unsubstantiated claims about environmental or health benefits. We explain our quality construction criteria, which goes beyond the code, and our building philosophy.

Green by Design

As a green builder, it is important that your clients understand the value of engaging your services at the start of the project. It is frustrating when potential clients contact us after they've begun the process of designing their new home, because when we prepare estimates for them we invariably notice omissions. We always have options and ideas for improving a plan's efficiency and reducing construction costs. However, redesigning a home to incorporate these changes can negate any savings that could have been achieved.

It's a good practice to meet prospective clients in the early stages to learn about their wants and needs. I generally invite an architect to participate in this initial meeting as well. Although I work with a number of architects, I am partial to those who have a proactive outlook on green building. For example, Tom Tyler, principle, Answers Inc., a Saint Louis architectural firm, designs homes that are actually five years ahead of the green market, in order to ensure that the project will still be cutting edge even after two years of design-build time. "We want to be on the leading edge of green, not the bleeding edge. By the time we take a project completely though the design build process, it is about three years ahead. That provides enough confidence that the technology is relevant and reliable" Tyler says.

After this initial meeting, your next meeting with the client should include trade contractors and suppliers, such as heating, ventilation, and air conditioning (HVAC) and insulation contractors, carpenters, and lumber companies. They are the experienced experts in their respective fields who can offer suggestions to simplify and expedite the construction process.

During this meeting we present innovative ways for the client to incorporate their needs and wants within their budgetary limitations. Then, we take extra steps to explain alternatives to increase the efficiency and sustainability of their new home. We usually present the client with an *à la carte* list of options, according to their home plan, to improve the overall performance of their home and still work within their budget.

We developed our list of options through comprehensive research by attending industry events such as the NAHB National Green Building Conference, USGBC'S Green Build (which has broadened its scope to include commercial as well as residential construction), specialty conferences such as the Energy and Environmental Building Association (EEBA) annual education symposium, and reading industry publications such as *Green Builder* magazine and *Green Building Product Dealer*.

OPTIONS FOR GREEN BUILDING

- Zoned heating and cooling
- High-efficiency air conditioning (14 Seasonal Energy Efficiency Ratio [SEER] minimum)
- High-efficiency furnace(s) (minimum 98% Annual Fuel Utilization Efficiency [AFUE])
- Geothermal system 50 gal. quick recovery gas water heater
  - Tankless water heater
- Individual air returns in each bedroom
- R-38 (approximate) blown ceiling insulation with no added formaldehyde
- Computerized panelized wall construction
- R-19 (approximate) spray cellulose insulation
- Advanced air sealing package featuring low Volatile Organic Compound (VOC) sealants
- Double-glazed, low-E (emissivity), argon-filled windows
- Water-conserving faucets and fixtures
- Passive radon mitigation system
- Solar synapse system

OPTIONS FOR GREEN BUILDING *(continued)*

- Home owner education to assure optimum performance of home and systems
- Low VOC framing and finish materials
- Recycled content ceramic tile in all wet areas
- Premium low VOC carpeting over ½"-high rebound pad in bedrooms
- Certified wood interior trim with low VOC finish
- Three coats of low VOC paint on interior walls with smooth finish
- Low VOC caulks and sealants throughout
- ENERGY STAR-rated bath exhaust fans
- Performance test of home to assure all systems function properly
- ENERGY STAR certification
- ¾" 50-year engineered wood subfloor
- 200-ampere electrical service with copper branch wiring
- 5-year "all inclusive" warranty
- Green building verification at no charge through the Green Building Initiative of St. Louis

Green Guidelines & Standards

There are approximately 60 green building programs and guidelines. The three most prevalent include *The National Green Building Standard* (ANSI ICC-700), U.S. Green Building Council's (USGBC) Leadership in Energy and Environmental Design (LEED) *LEED for Homes* (*LEED-H*), and the Green Building Initiative's (GBI) *Green Globes* for commercial buildings.

National Green Building Standard

The *NAHB Model Green Building Guidelines* were the basis for the *ICC-700 2008 National Green Building Standard,* the national green rating system endorsed collaboratively by the International Code Council (ICC) and NAHB. The Standard was approved by the American National Standards Institute (ANSI) in January 2009.

The Standard describes the green practices that can be incorporated into new homes, including multi-family buildings, home renovations and additions, and larger site development projects, such as green subdivisions.

The Standard has four performance levels—Bronze, Silver, Gold, and Emerald—that provide builders with a means to achieve everything from basic, entry-level green building, to the highest level of sustainable "green" building that incorporates energy savings of 60% or higher. In order to earn threshold level points, a green home must achieve a minimum score in each of the following categories:

1. Lot Design, preparation, and development
2. Resource efficiency
3. Energy efficiency
4. Water efficiency
5. Indoor environmental quality
6. Operation, maintenance, and building owner education

Bronze

Homes built today are 100% more energy efficient that those constructed in past generations, so most builders just need a little nudge to go into other green areas. The Bronze level of green building allows builders to "dip their toes in the pool of green building." This level of green has exponentially expanded the market for green building and the number of affordable green homes built. As builders become more familiar and comfortable with green practices, competition and consumer awareness will increase, and as a result builders can reach for higher levels of green construction.

Silver

This level of the *National Green Building Standard* gives a deeper leap into the green pool; its requirements are similar to LEED-H. If you comply with the upper tier of the Silver level, you probably already qualify for an ENERGY STAR rating too. In addition to helping the environment, having both ratings can be a great attribute to trumpet in marketing your homes.

Gold

If you build within this level, you probably already comply with other standards such as ENERGY STAR, the U.S. Environmental Protection Agency's (EPA) Water Sense, and LEED-H. This level also provides a unique marketing opportunity.

Emerald

This level is the top tier for residential green construction and signifies "raising the bar" for builders. As new technology enters the market and builders improve their construction practices, the Emerald level will allow builders who achieve it to differentiate themselves in the marketplace.

Overall the Standard has higher thresholds than the older Guidelines. The Standard takes into account current code requirements more comprehensively. For example, in the Guidelines if you vented your bath exhaust you were awarded basic points for doing so, even though some local building codes may have required you to do so anyway. Under the Standard, that venting is mandatory with no points awarded. The Standard also references the 2006 International Energy Conservation Code (IECC). To reach the Bronze level requires a minimum scale of 15% above the 2006 IECC in the energy section, which is also equivalent to ENERGY STAR.

The Standard also addresses how builders can incorporate sensible green protocols into larger homes. The thresholds vary depending on the relative size of the home; larger homes are penalized with additional requirements. Obviously, larger homes require more materials and use more energy than smaller homes, but building in accordance with these adjusted thresholds will soften the impact these homes would have if they were built using traditional methods.

The Standard also identifies and allows inclusion of different levels of remodeling and additions, by delineating different requirements depending on the scope of the project. This will allow remodelers to benefit from the focused efficiency that the Standard requires.

Using the Guidelines, Belcher Homes has strengthened our focus on better building (and better building business) practices. We believed, rightly so, that our philosophy and processes meant we were doing a good job; but, after we increased our focus on reducing construction waste, we were able to reduce it by almost 70%, or approximately two dumpster loads of waste per house. At a rate of $350 per dumpster to transport the waste to the landfill, the cost savings were as significant as the positive environmental impact. We also save on materials costs, labor time, cleanup, and dumping fees, and we have the personal satisfaction of knowing that we send far less waste to the landfill. Our customers appreciate our efforts as well—we have a reputation for being an environmentally responsible company.

Meanwhile, as the *National Green Building Standard* becomes more widely recognized, builders can expect it to eventually become more widely used and referenced, creating a paradigm shift in the home building industry. As standards become more known, builders already familiar with green building will definitely have a competitive advantage.

Leadership in Energy and Environmental Design Program (LEED)

The USGBC's LEED program, a well-established brand in commercial building, added the LEED for Homes (LEED-H) program in 2007. LEED-H has four levels of certification:

1. Certified
2. Silver
3. Gold
4. Platinum

Certified is similar to the *National Green Building Standard's* Bronze level; Silver and Gold are comparable to the Standard's Silver and Gold levels; and, the Platinum level equates to the Emerald level in the Standard.

Builders must not lose sight of the customer's best interest in seeking validation through either the

National Green Building Standard or *LEED-H*. Avoid getting so caught up in chasing the necessary points to achieve a given level of green performance at the expense of your customer, who is relying on your professional expertise to guide them through the green building process. Your reputation and the home's price tag are among the top concerns in the customer's home buying decision. You can build a home to the Emerald or Platinum level, but if the customer cannot afford it, what have you really achieved?

Belcher Homes has achieved Platinum certification in the LEED-H program, and Gold certifications in our local HBA program. Our local Realtor® association's multiple listing service recently adopted a new checklist for homes that reflects the *Green Building Standard*, LEED-H, ENERGY STAR, and a list of green features. Appraisers can use this tool when examining homes for banks and mortgage lenders. Tools such as this provide quantifiable information so when my customers are ready to invest some of their home equity into completing that solar power system that their home was prewired for, they will reap the benefits of the additional equity these highly rated homes carry.

The upshot for builders is that as the *National Green Building Standard* and the LEED-H programs progress, if you build to one, you will generally be able to comply with the other, and you will most likely qualify for the ENERGY STAR rating also.

In 2006, we built a home for the Engelmohrs who wanted to design and build under the LEED-H program and the NAHB Guidelines. Maren Engelmohr is a licensed architect. She was on the design team for Alberici Corp. headquarters, which is considered to be one of the greenest commercial buildings in the world. She also led the design for her family's home. Although the LEED-H program was still in its pilot stage, the basics were established. Some of the nomenclature evolved in the LEED-H pilot program during the planning and construction phases; however, quite a few of the changes reflected requirements of the NAHB Guidelines, which made it easier to coordinate both criteria.

But the most important factor for us as the Engelmohrs' builder was that they knew they wanted to build their new home green to create a healthy environment for their two young children. Their current house was over 100 years old and had all the characteristics of a home that age—good and bad. The Engelmohrs are prototypical buyers of a green home: They wanted a home that was energy efficient, durable, built with a softer environmental footprint, and constructed to promote a healthier lifestyle.

Our firm had just purchased a small development in Kirkwood, Mo., a suburb of St. Louis. The Engelmohrs selected a lot that would accommodate an appropriately sized home and take advantage of good solar orientation. We started with a preliminary design and established how the home would be situated on the lot. After considering different budget options for building materials and systems, we decided upon structural insulated panels (SIPs) for the walls and roof (fig. 1). We started the house in January, when it can and did get very cold during framing; the high temperature was four degrees when we set the roof panels. However, once all the panels were set, the walls and roof were sheeted and insulated due to the SIPs, so we were able to close the window and door rough openings and complete the interior framing and rough in while we were wearing shirt sleeves.

Green Building Initiative (GBI)

The GBI is a national nonprofit organization devoted to advancing green building. GBI promotes its own commercial program, Green Globes, a green management tool that includes an assessment protocol, a rating system, and a guide for integrating environmentally friendly design into commercial buildings. GBI was helpful in launching the Green Building Initiative, St. Louis (GBI-STL) under the auspices of the St. Louis Home Builders Association (HBA).

Specifically, the GBI helped the St. Louis HBA develop a program to educate and train builders and verifiers through classroom and field instruction to identify and verify that the guidelines are being followed. The classroom instruction provides a comprehensive explanation of the guidelines and the point system used to determine performance levels. The field instruction provides the trainees an opportunity

Figure 1. Engelmohr residence

The walls and the roof of the home were constructed using SIPs, a process in which the panels are laid out and numbered in order of installation.

to identify and verify the criteria that was presented in the classroom in actual homes under various stages of construction. The training is also available online. To learn more about the GBI, visit their Web site at http://www.thegbi.org.

The verifiers impartially evaluate green building projects in order to level the playing field for all green home builders and inspire consumer confidence. Although St. Louis HBA members had considered verifying each other's work, this verification option was dismissed because of concerns about sharing proprietary information, the necessary time commitment, and credibility with consumers and other external groups. We determined that an independent, third-party verifier was the best choice.

HBAs that would like to consider a similar program can find third-party verifiers through home energy rating specialists (HERS) and home inspectors. Our local gas utility, The Laclede Gas Company's Alternative Energy Engineering Group volunteered their services to serve as our verifier. The Green Building Initiative also brought in trainers to train Laclede's engineers to gather the information required to verify homes according to the NAHB's green guidelines checklist and to use building plans; site visits; vendor-supplied data, such as material safety data sheets; and job site inspection logs to check information such as moisture content in wood, to verify compliance. Laclede's process is a national model for developing a verification process, and has earned the company a positive reputation as a public utility that promotes energy and building efficiency.

The NAHB has also established and trained a national network of certified verifiers through its National Green Building Program. The USGBC has also worked to establish certifiers across the nation and are available in limited numbers.

Thanks to the efforts of our Green Building Council and staff, the St. Louis HBA now has a process that makes its green building program a resource for its members who want to build green. In 2007, the St. Louis HBA's Green Building Council gained national recognition when it received NAHB's New Program of the Year award for the best new green program. In 2008, we were recognized as the Best Association Program for its Members by NAHB.

In the following chapters I will share some of my company's most successful green building projects, so you can see how easily you can incorporate green building techniques into your future projects.

CHAPTER 2

BUILDING HOMES
THAT LAST

Sustainability entails a commitment to design and construct buildings and spaces that reduce the demand on nonrenewable resources and help preserve environmental quality. Sustainable design requires builders to meet current needs, without compromising the availability of resources for future generations.

"When speaking about the sustainability of a home or building you are speaking about the future of that building," says Thomas Taylor, general manager of Vertegy, a green building consulting firm. In other words, builders must *future-proof* the homes they build to stand the test of time.

We must consider the following:

- How sustainable is the building?
- How easily can it be upgraded?
- Can it be adapted to future technologies without difficulty?

For example, it is customary for builders to offer a future-proof electronics package, so that phones, computers, and other similar devices can be upgraded as new innovations in technology occur.

Green builders who future-proof their homes tend to work with architects who develop relevant designs, so a home's functions do not become obsolete. For example, sustainable design includes prewiring the home for solar power, so that it can be incrementally adapted as various solar technologies emerge on the market. Currently solar installations are cost prohibitive for new homes, especially in northern states.

However, prewiring the home for solar so that it will be readily available for future installations is very easy and cost effective. Buildings that are wired to harvest sunlight use solar panels to capture the sun's power to produce AC current for general household use. This free, renewable energy is of a higher quality than that produced by an electric utility, and generating it produces no pollution. Inverters can convert DC power to AC power. Moreover, solar photovoltaic power systems continue to decrease in cost. Their price has fallen considerably since the 1970s. As the cost of installing the equipment decreases, the market for solar systems continues to grow. Solar power epitomizes the concept of sustainability (fig. 2).

Green housing is built to go the distance, because it is more robust than traditional housing. From better design and engineering to superior materials and construction methods, green housing is built for durability. For example, green homes may be built using vinyl or fiber cement siding, both of which are sturdy, long lasting, and decrease the home owner's energy use and maintenance costs. Green construction materials, such as asbestos-free components and nontoxic glues, can be completely recycled. By using more efficient products, fixtures, and equipment in housing, builders can decrease the demand on energy and water supplies and other natural resources, and save the home owner money.

By using more efficient products, fixtures and equipment in housing, builders can decrease the demand on energy and water supplies and other natural resources, and save the home owner money.

When Belcher Homes begins a project, we envision the future house on its site and every component that will go into the house as one system to be planned and built for sustainability.

Components such as wood, concrete, shingles, an HVAC system, flooring, and other common components comprise most homes. With a systems approach to green building, we measure each component's impact on the environment and look for

Figure 2. Solar synapse box

This is the type of solar synapse prewire design that Belcher Homes incorporates into its homes. This box is typically installed the attic or upper level of a home.

green alternatives. For example, we might replace traditional framing with SIPs. Although SIPs can be more expensive than traditional framing, some savvy home buyers realize the long-term benefits of superior insulating quality and structural durability they provide. Using SIPs may allow installation of a smaller HVAC system as well, saving or at least offsetting the cost of using SIPs.

A systems approach can also extend to a home's plumbing design. By placing all of the rooms that use plumbing in proximity, you can reduce the size of the plumbing system, thereby reducing the amount of materials (such as piping) needed and the distance hot water must flow and, therefore, the energy needed to heat it. In the Engelmohrs' two-story home, for example, we centrally located the kitchen, laundry room, and all bathrooms near each other. We were able to serve all of the client's hot water needs with one properly sized tankless water heater (fig. 3).

Even something as simple as changing the types of framing materials you use and the way you use them can make your homes more green. A typical home is constructed or framed with nominal 2 × 4 stud framing (which actually measure 1½ in. × 3½ in.) located 16 in. apart on center or 14½ in. apart edge to edge. Changing to a 2 × 6 stud and decreasing the spacing to 24 in. on center helps save materials while providing added insulation (fig. 4). You can increase the thickness of insulation system used in exterior walls while decreasing the amount of stud material

Figure 3. Tankless water heater

This tankless water heater provides all of the hot water needed for the home.

Figure 4. 2 × 6 framing

Using 2 × 6 construction allows more room for insulation and allows studs to be spaced further apart reducing thermal bridging.

needed. You will maintain good structural integrity because your roof trusses typically are spaced 2 ft. apart, the spacing lines up directly under each roof truss.

Good Site Planning is Key

Environmentally sound site planning is the first step to sustainable development. We all know the tenets of real estate: location, location, location. For a green deve-lopers, selecting the right location is just as important as knowing which locations to avoid. The qualities to consider when selecting a site are as follows:

- solar orientation
- topography
- soil analysis
- water conservation analysis
- trees and other existing foliage
- site limitations

After selecting a site, green builders assess how best to work the site and protect its natural features. One of the biggest mistakes builders can make is to select a beautiful site and not take advantage of its natural beauty, or worse, destroy it.

Solar Orientation

Solar orientation, or orienting the house to the sun's path, is key to successful site planning. If you can find a site where you can take advantage of passive solar heating and cooling, you have tapped into something truly amazing: free energy (at least nobody has figured out how to tax sunshine yet, anyway). A well-designed and properly oriented house capitalizes on solar heat gain in winter and deflects unwanted heat in summer. This simple consideration can measurably lower a home's energy use—and at no extra cost (fig. 5).

Figure 5. Angle of the sun

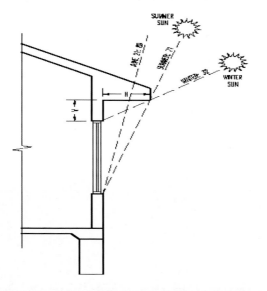

Properly designing overhang allow you to take advantage of the seasonal angles of the sun. This should be one of your first design considerations.

When we develop housing sites, Belcher Homes takes full advantage of solar orientation. When we design lot layout, we plot the path of the sun in relation to the home sites. This simple consideration can save a healthy percentage of a house's energy use—and at no extra cost.

From a development standpoint, we want to plan the location and orientation of each house in relation to its neighbors, so that two-story homes will not shade ranch-style models, for example, which would prevent the one-story homes' future use of solar energy. There is nothing you can do to increase a home's value so much for such a small investment in planning (figs. 6, 7).

Figure 6.   Homes sited side-by-side

These two homes were sited so that the home on the left (south) would not obstruct the ability of the home on the right (north) to receive solar panels on its roof.

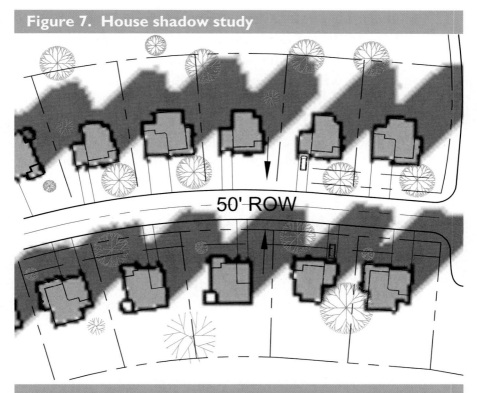

Figure 7. House shadow study

50' ROW

This is a typical plot plan over which we impose a computerized solar path showing how shadows will fall as the sun crosses the lot or development. This allows us to plan the sales and placement of homes in relation to each other.

Once we select a site, decide which home plan is best, and orient that home according to the sun's path, we then incorporate design features and materials that will further maximize the home's use of solar energy. For example, placing stone and brick walls or decorative features, or fireplace and chimney on the south wall is a green design concept known as *thermal mass*. These surfaces can absorb and retain the sun's heat in the winter and, after dark, radiate heat back into the house. This is a good example of passive solar design, which makes the most of the sun's power to lower heating costs.

During the summer, if you have oriented the house properly and are able to take advantage of shade trees and overhangs, (shading the aforementioned thermal mass and the windows) the air conditioner has cooler air to work with—approximately 20° cooler than it would be otherwise.

Proper solar orientation can also provide glare-free natural light throughout the house, especially with contemporary design techniques such as incorporating light-colored surfaces, using glass partitions, and applying other light maximizing techniques. These techniques reduce the need for artificial lighting, which saves electricity and lowers the amount of heat generated in the home, decreasing the need for air-conditioning in the summer. Passive solar design is one very effective way of harnessing the sun's power to enhance the energy efficiency of your house. Although it is desirable to limit Northern facing glazing, incorporating a balance of daylight from the North usually results in a more constant "softer" natural light.

When my dad built the house I grew up in, he positioned it to take advantage of the sun's warmth in wintertime (fig. 8). In the summer, the house received maximum shading from overhangs and from the surrounding trees. As the following photo shows, the shadow of the overhang bisects the wall right in the middle, at noon, on the Vernal Equinox.

Sunlight is abundant and freely distributed all over our planet's surface.

Figure 8. Overhang of childhood home

Designed to allow for passive gain in wintertime and to assist with shading in summertime, the overhang worked just as intended, because the house site essentially plotted the path of the sun.

Topography

Topography is the lay of the land. A topographic map of a site shows the relative position and elevation of the natural features of the landscape. A good topographic map, combined with a builder's assessment after walking a site, promotes using a site wisely and preserving and conserving its natural elements to the fullest extent possible. You must understand fully a site's features before removing trees, if necessary, and grading.

On a custom home site or a larger development site in particular, this thorough assessment allows builders to situate a home in a way that minimizes tree clearing, lessening environmental impact and saving the builder money. Contrary to popular belief, builders do not want to carelessly bulldoze trees. Besides the fact that builders enjoy the natural environment as much as everyone else, each time we touch a tree, we have to pay to do something with it.

Another reason builders need a topographic view of a site is to see how much grading will be required. Again, by limiting the amount of grading, builders can minimize their impact on the land and lower costs.

Topographic maps combined with a live site assessment are useful in developing site plans because they help builders answer the following questions:

- What is the best location for the house, out-buildings, and driveways?

- How should the house be positioned among the trees?
- How can the natural aesthetics of the site be maximized?
- Where are the rock outcroppings?
- How can the removal of trees and other natural features of the landscape be limited?

A good topographic map allows builders to use a site wisely and preserve and conserve its natural elements to the fullest extent possible.

Our Labarque Creek Watershed site offers a good example of the value of topographic maps in developing site plans (fig. 9). The residence constructed on this site won the first Gold Level Green Home Verification in St. Louis, Missouri, from the HBA of Greater St. Louis and Eastern Missouri in 2007. The site had two large waterways or *draws* on it. We positioned the house away from the larger draw, assuming any storm water runoff migrating into it would have a large and almost immediate impact on the community lake immediately below our home site as well as on the wider watershed. When correctly directed, however, natural storm water can become an added amenity.

Soil Analysis

The objective of soil analysis is to limit surprises such as rock, plastic soils, and other challenging site conditions during a project. The more educated the developer is about site conditions before turning over

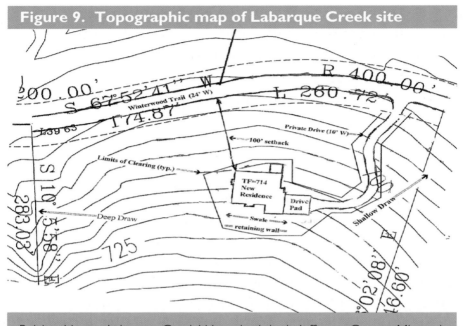

Figure 9. Topographic map of Labarque Creek site

Belcher Homes Labarque Creek Watershed site in Jefferson County, Missouri, January 2006.

a shovel, the better the outcome of a project will be. Therefore it is important to examine soils in advance to see how they will respond. Clays respond very differently from sands. Clays absorb water and swell, which could result in heaving and cracking of footings or foundation walls; whereas, sands tend to liquefy when saturated making them useless for bearing upon. Therefore, they require different building techniques. Knowledge of soil types on a site helps the entire project team maintain control of the building process and ultimately achieve the desired outcome.

When Belcher Homes excavates a foundation, we hire a soils engineer to examine soil samples and verify that our design will work on the site. The minimal cost, approximately $100, for this "ounce of prevention," is worth heading off the potential headaches that future soil-related problems might cause (for which $100 would not buy enough aspirin to cure!).

As we remove the topsoil, we stockpile it on-site. When the excavation and rough grading in the subsurface soils is complete, we use the topsoil for finish grading. We strive to avoid mixing clays and other undesirable soils with the topsoil unless we need to amend some of the undesirable soils with that topsoil.

I took a soils engineering class a number of years ago to learn more about this aspect of construction. As a result, I have an increased appreciation for the importance of soils in building sustainable housing, and I understand the importance of soils engineers. (By the way, I was never as happy to get a "B" in my life as I was after that class. It was tough!)

Water Conservation Analysis

Good water conservation analysis is an important part of low-impact development (LID). It creates a homestead or entire development that handles storm water properly and can also help enhance wildlife habitat by providing sources of food and water for birds and other wildlife.

The purpose of water conservation analysis is to identify wetlands, floodplains, and tributaries, and

avoid adversely affecting these areas in home construction. An awareness of the natural water flows of
the property, allows builders to design a lot layout that
complements the way nature handles storm water.

On a single-site custom development, the builder
can easily perform a water conservation analysis
simply by walking the site. On a larger site, builders
should create a natural resources inventory map by
walking the site, studying photos and topographic
maps of the area, and making surveys. Then incorporate that map into the concept plan map as part of
site planning.

In our own site planning, Belcher Homes' overall
layouts are based on natural water flows, which are
different for each property. Because of our approach,
which respects what nature wants to do; we build drier
homes and basements while allowing for efficient
handling of storm water.

As part of our low-impact and sustainable development techniques, we use underground cisterns to
catch roof runoff and pipe that harvested rainwater
to an in-ground drip irrigation system. A 1¼ in. rainfall on a 1,000 sq. ft. roof produces approximately
150 gallons of water.

Bioswales

Whenever possible, we incorporate *bioswales* (vegetated ditches) into our site design to serve as catch-
ment basins for storm water from the roof, yard, and

street. Bioswales are designed to allow water to flow at a controlled rate and to help filter the storm water. They can absorb huge amounts of storm water and efficiently move the water around, which helps to control flooding and reduces runoff. In conjunction with other types of rainwater-collection systems, bioswales help create natural habitat for many plant and wildlife species and beautify neighborhoods. They also can serve as an artificially created but beneficial watershed in urban areas. In essence, bioswales help close the water loop.

When Belcher Homes creates bioswales, we plant them with native species that will thrive in them, including indigenous grasses and wildflowers. Unlike lawn turf, which is bred for regular watering and moist ground and, as a result, develops only shallow roots that trap very little storm water, native prairie grasses and plants evolved naturally to have deep, tough roots that anchor the soil. Their roots can extend 8 to 12 ft. underground or even deeper, seeking out water sources that enable the plants to survive drought and other hardships. Moreover, their assorted heights, blooming seasons, colors, textures, and leaf architecture present a glorious panorama year-round that is as aesthetically pleasing as it is functional.

Figure 10 depicts a rough graded *swale* or *constructed wetland*. It was designed to catch and slow storm water runoff, allowing plant and soil enhancement materials to absorb and filter the water. Because

Figure 10. Constructed wetland

The details in the grading create a pool at the upper end to slow water so that it is filtered as it meanders through the wetland.

of its location at the low end of the site, it serves as a *silt trap* until upstream drainage areas are planted and vegetated. Afterward it is cleaned out, finish graded, and planted.

In one project we consulted on, the grading contractor used a biodiesel-powered D-9 bulldozer with GPS pods on its blades to create the detailed grading (fig. 11). The contours were loaded into the GPS

Figure 11. GPS bulldozer with pods

Using technology even in heavy equipment during the grading process saves resources and time. I never dreamed of such things as a kid pushing my Tonka trucks around my jobsite (sandbox). This is like a Tonka truck on steroids!

system and the operator simply navigated through the area as satellites controlled the angle and depth of grades. It took about four hours to complete a process that otherwise would have taken significantly longer and burned more fuel.

In development design, we work with ecological engineers who use bioswales in place of storm sewers, which are engineered so storm water that falls on site is slowed and treated on site. Any water that does manage to leave the site will be cleaner than when it fell, thanks to the bioswale systems.

You will need to plan to include these features into your overall storm water control plan well in advance. Use your best management practices (BMPs) to stipulate that the rain garden is supposed to exist on the lot, and your indentures or covenants to protect the rain garden's existence. Therefore, if a particular rain garden is located on an individual lot and that lot is resold in the future the new owner cannot alter or eliminate the rain garden. Be sure to post your BMPs in common areas or other community spaces, so that home owner associations, or similar entities, can better manage the maintenance of the rain gardens. This should be particularly appealing to municipal entities, because it means that in 30 years or so, they will not have to maintain storm sewer systems. Instead of storm sewer maintenance crews, a few steadfast gardeners will do!

Trees and Existing Foliage

As responsible builders, our job is to work with nature, not against it. Mother Nature has done a pretty good job with site layout. Therefore, builders should strive to incorporate natural features such as existing trees and other foliage into their site plans whenever possible. These natural elements often enhance the value of the site and help with solar shading, which saves money for the builder and the home buyer.

Belcher Homes uses low-impact and conservation development techniques that are designed to save as many trees on a site as possible. On smaller sites, we select and clear trees by hand, starting in the middle of the site and felling trees toward the center to avoid damaging unharvested trees. We grind out stumps and sell any marketable timber or use it for firewood. We use mulch made from the harvested trees to mix with the stockpiled topsoil that is removed prior to excavating of the foundation. Some trees may become a safety hazard to the home owner and the arborist helps us identify those as well (fig. 12).

When construction is complete, we grade the land around the house with a finish layer of the conserved topsoil and decomposed mulch. This creates a good planting area that is very permeable and slows storm water, allowing the site to absorb water and reducing runoff. In our Labarque creek project, this practice helped control runoff tremendously mitigating any impact our construction may have had on the watershed.

Overcoming Site Limitations

Sometimes a site has an apparent limitation that turns out to be a unique design opportunity. For example, a creek, cliff, or rock outcropping can enhance the beauty or function of a site and create a dramatic backdrop. In general, Belcher Homes tends to view site limitations as a doorway to site enhancement, rather than a barrier to site design.

Figure 12. Mature trees saved

Plot plan on left shows storm sewer and catch basin required by local ordinance to be installed sub-surface in lieu of bioretention or bioswales on lot 1. If located where shown, it would have eliminated a stand of mature trees. We were able to get permission to amend the footprint of the home located on lot 1, move the garage to the rear and move the easement for the sewer line over to save the stand of trees (shown in photo on right). Our arborist was onsite to oversee excavation to minimize impact on the trees.

For example, I built a home for my brother and sister-in-law a few years ago. They had purchased a lot that most builders would recognize as "difficult." It dropped from the building line steeply to the valley floor way below, and they designed a very deep house to build on it. However, by using careful soils exploration and excavation, we were able to pin the foundation to solid rock (which, fortunately was at the perfect depth). We managed to minimally disturb the site and existing mature trees. As a result, they have a scenic view from their great room and deck and they enjoy maximum shading from the remaining mature trees in the summertime.

As responsible builders, it is important that we use natural resources wisely so that they will be available for future generations. We know how to make decisions that are financially sound; now it is important that we make environmentally sound decisions as well.

3

USING RESOURCES WISELY

When constructing a sustainable house, green developers are very conscientious of using resources wisely. We take a holistic approach to development that looks to the future. In my experience, such an approach also benefits the bottom line, because eco-friendly construction practices save money. Not only has Belcher Homes saved money by utilizing better materials and more efficient waste management techniques, we've received major kudos from consumers and community groups because our building practices reduce amount of waste sent to landfills.

Reducing, Recycling, Reusing

As builders we are blessed with the ability to create an opportunity for a potential home buyer to live the American Dream. But making the dream a reality requires us to use natural resources. To be good stewards of the Earth and the materials we use to perform our craft, we must use those resources as efficiently as possible. The good news is that there are constantly emerging technologies that will allow us to do just that.

For example, the timber industry now grows and harvests trees more sustainably. With hybrids and new biotechnologies, timber companies can bring young trees to harvest size in just 8 years, instead of the 24 to 25 years it usually takes for trees to mature. Further, timber companies largely grow their crops on tree farms, or in sustainably managed forests, that don't damage native forests and habitats.

In addition to operating tree farms, these companies now manage forests better and preserve natural systems as much as possible when they harvest mature trees. Their sustainable harvesting methods can also improve woodlands, because they remove diseased and dead trees and keep undergrowth in check, which lessens the risk of fires and opens up glade areas for healthy young trees and wildlife. Even most loggers would agree that the sustainability of the future of their jobs depends on it.

Lumber suppliers marketing to green builders support sustainable timber harvesting by selling Forest Stewardship Council (FSC) or Sustainable Forestry

Initiative (SFI) certified lumber. Both certifications are recognized by the NAHB Green Building Program. Currently, LEED-H only recognizes FSC certification.

Many timber producing states such as Oregon also have laws that dictate how timber can be harvested, including how loggers may enter and traverse forests, streams, and other natural habitat, so workers leave a softer footprint. Manufacturers associated with the timber industry are inventing new technology to improve forest management. For example, John Deere has developed a machine, the Timberjack Harvester that literally walks through a forest on legs instead of traveling on wheels or tracks. It has computer controlled sensors that plant the feet and if a soft spot is detected in the forest floor, the Timberjack will lift and reset that foot.

Computerized satellite imagery is used to identify harvestable areas in managed forests to prevent wasted time and timber. The path to traverse the forest to these areas can be identified to have the least impact possible.

The lumber industry is also looking to help focus certification efforts by developing programs to stamp lumber in the same manner it is now stamped according to grade. This would allow the lumber to be identified as a sustainable product all the way from harvesting through the construction process. In the distant future, when a building may be deconstructed, the sustainable identification would live on. I like the idea of having my clients (and potential clients) walk through one of our framed homes and see a sustainably harvested stamp on every stick of lumber. What a great sales tool!

We take advantage of all these new industry efficiencies by partnering with our materials suppliers. For example, once we determine what we need for a project, our suppliers cut and size components to fit before they deliver them to the site. Therefore, we only pay for what we use. As a result, the earliest we bring a dumpster to the jobsite for scrap is at the drywall stage, which indicates how little we waste when we build. If we could get drywall manufacturers and health regulators on board, perhaps we wouldn't need a dumpster at all.

We prefer having materials precut and presized for the following reasons:

1. We don't want to spend our time (time is money!) cutting to fit on site and picking up scrap.
2. We don't want to purchase more than we need.
3. We want to build in a sustainable manner.

It all boils down to making the most efficient use of limited resources while improving quality. This practice also allows us to cut framing time by about half, so we are weathered in sooner, which helps with moisture management.

This approach helps Belcher Homes design more sustainable housing. Because we coordinate all plumbing design with an eye toward creating shorter pipe runs, for example, we can buy far less plumbing material, which helps lower expenses and reduces our use of resources. As you might imagine, the cumulative effect of such thoughtful design work has proven to be much more efficient for the home owner as well.

We are currently exploring the feasibility of shipping unused and scrap drywall back to the supplier to grind and reuse to produce new drywall, thereby virtually eliminating any drywall waste.

We also plan to provide ground scrap lumber shavings to horse stables as bedding. This is possible now because toxins are no longer used in manufacturing the lumber we use. The stables will recycle the used bedding as compost mulch, since it will be mixed with organic material, courtesy of the horses. We can then take the decomposed shavings mixed with the organic materials and use them in our community gardens and plant areas.

Belcher Homes takes this holistic approach to its building projects because our definition of success includes sustaining natural resources well into the future.

Enhancing Durability and Reducing Maintenance

Enhancing durability, by definition, reduces maintenance and the expenses associated with it. This concept is important for green builders, who seek to construct sustainable housing, and for home owners, who want livable houses that will stand the test of time. In durability and in every other area of home building, Belcher Homes continues to exceed its previous standards, thanks in part to the green movement, which has led to a renaissance in building science.

In our quest to build more durable homes, Belcher Homes uses more engineered lumber today than ever before. Engineered lumber is prevalent in the market. When trees can be grown to harvestable size in only eight years it affects the log itself. Imagine the growth rings you would see in a cross section of a 16-in. diameter log. Can you imagine that same log with only eight rings? This means the log is less dense. However, when you grind and compress it at high pressure and combine it with nontoxic epoxies, the end product is a wood composite that is stronger than its traditional dimensional counterpart from that same log!

These new methods have led to a change in building codes during the last few code cycles. Builders, especially green builders, are now incorporating more engineered lumber in the construction process; however, the codes still recognize that less dense dimensional lumber is also used. As a result of seemingly more frequent natural disasters involving wind damage, more emphasis is being required in structural and wind shear design with an eye toward building components.

At Belcher Homes, our framing practices are better as well. The combination of engineered lumber and sound practices produces a framework of greater strength with less warping. This is just one example of how builders can maximize housing durability and efficient use of materials—imagine multiplying this effect across the entire house! Essentially you will have created a home that is easier and less expensive to maintain, which in turn helps increase the value of the house as an asset for the home owner (fig. 13).

At Belcher Homes we've learned that building for durability allows us to foster a better relationship with our customers. This approach to home construction also gives us a healthier bottom line and the satisfaction of knowing we contribute to sustaining

Figure 13. Cultured stone

This stone is made of lightweight concrete. It provides a durable, attractive, exterior finish. It costs less than real stone to install and it is completely recyclable.

ecosystems. After all, we need natural resources to build houses, as will generations of builders to come, so it is clearly in our own self-interest to conserve these resources and use them wisely.

Organizations such as the Energy and Environmental Building Association (EEBA), a building science group that publishes guides detailing all aspects of housing construction such as proper ways to flash doors and windows, etc., have boosted our quality and the industry to a new level. It is important to stay abreast of what organizations such as EEBA, NAHB, USGBSC and others are doing to foster green building techniques by reading their green-related publications and attending their green conferences. When I attend conferences, I learn a lot by just walking the exhibits floor and visiting vendors.

Reusing and Recycling Materials

Of course, there will always be some waste associated with using materials. One approach to minimizing both the amount of waste generated and the amount that gets dumped in landfills is to view housing as part of a broader manufacturing cycle. At Belcher Homes we think the waste materials of construction—and in due course the components of the home itself—should all be reincorporated into new manufacturing cycles.

Our objective as green builders, therefore, is to operate as if we can throw nothing away and as if everything we build must eventually be recovered for reuse and recycling. Builders must employ efficient design and planning strategies that minimize the use of materials and maximize durability to create homes that in time can be deconstructed, and the materials used to build the home can be recycled and reused.

For example, the foundation of the Engelmohr's home was designed to receive the engineered floor system. The engineered floor joists spanned from wall-to-wall without the need of an intermediate steel beam. We were able to order specific lengths of engineered joists for this application thereby eliminating any cut off waste.

This philosophy is becoming more and more a reality as resources, especially natural resources, become strained and more scarce. As this occurs, all of the materials that were customarily considered waste will increase in economic value, and recovery and reuse will be a mainstay of the residential construction business.

We identify sources of waste and address them before they arrive at the jobsite. When materials are left over, there are several ways builders can reuse and recycle them. During construction, we recycle as much waste as we can. We work with a company that collects our roof shingle waste and grinds it to create a waterproofing spray from the recycled product that provides superior protection for our homes' foundations. We generate minimal metal scrap and recycle all of it. We grind drywall waste, which because of its gypsum content (hydrous calcium sulfate), could be spread on fields as a soil amendment, when permitted by local jurisdictions. It can also be recycled for use as Plaster of Paris.

At Belcher Homes we move scrap lumber to other jobsites for reuse, rather than discard it. Why buy new lumber to block and brace when we can reuse scrap? When we are finished with blocking and bracing and other scrap lumber we strip any nails or other hardware from it and give it to a local scout leader who recycles it into his scout troop's projects. In addition to these efforts, Belcher Homes is always seeking opportunities to work with local recycling centers for other types of construction waste.

When we purchase cabinetry, we reuse the cardboard packaging to protect floors, handrails, and other vulnerable parts of the house during construction. The amount of materials that arrive at a jobsite in cardboard cartons and packaging is amazing. After the final clean up, we transport the packaging to a recycling center, rather than a dumpster where it would only degrade and consume space.

In fact, we have a very organized process for collecting waste materials. Storage areas, units and bins are available in a designated area of the construction site that is easily accessible, even in inclement weather. Our highly visible waste collection area sends a strong message to regulatory agencies, our customers, and our construction crews that Belcher Homes is serious about sustainability.

As part of our "reuse and recycle" philosophy, we also look for recycled content whenever we purchase materials. This includes countertop materials, flooring tiles, wall coverings, and carpet. Our goal is to always increase the use of recycled, durable materials in building a house.

Using Renewable Materials

Lumber is a prime example of a renewable resource. As long as the timber industry manages its hardwood and whitewood tree farms and new-growth forests wisely, it can produce all the lumber we need without depleting our natural stocks or infringing on designated wilderness areas.

In addition to hardwoods and whitewoods, our customers occasionally request that we use bamboo. In those cases, we use materials such as Plyboo®, a bamboo-plywood in veneer form, for flooring that is more durable than bamboo. Although bamboo, a grass, is fast-growing and readily renewable, it is not native to our area. It is grown overseas, typically in Southeast Asia and other tropical locations. Therefore, it requires more energy to transport the bamboo to the United States and distribute it than if we had a local supply. Further, many developing countries have begun to strip their bamboo forests to satisfy world demand, thereby ruining their land and setting up landslide conditions.

The Four "R's" of Green
Building:
Reduce, reuse, recycle,
renew!

In contrast to bamboo, a renewable resource, gravel, which is used in to produce concrete, is a nonrenewable resource. We can decrease the amount of gravel that is mined by recycling concrete, crushing it for use in manufacturing new concrete and other products (fig. 14). Similarly, we can substitute Cambria, and other fabricated products, in place of granite in countertops.

Using Indigenous Materials

We try to use materials that are local to our area, or *local source,* as much as possible. In Missouri and northern Arkansas, we have one of the best-managed hardwood forests in North America, and it is the source of some of the lumber we use in construction. As a result, our costs are lower. Local sourcing helps lower pollution and energy consumption, which contributes to increasing resource productivity, economic efficiency, and local job creation.

Whenever we use local sources for natural resources and materials, manufactured products, transportation, energy and food, we are behaving in a manner that is self-sustaining and efficient. For example, in one home we used oak hardwood flooring from a local forest. We used a job-finished red oak in

Figure 14. Scoop of clean gravel

This scoop of clean gravel, which we use for granular fill under concrete slabs, etc. is actually crushed concrete. After deconstruction of an existing residence, the concrete slabs and foundation are crushed. We reuse it in lieu of crushed rock.

the common areas and white oak in the bedrooms. To date, I think it is one of the most beautiful floors in any home I have built.

Essentially, when we local source, we get more product for less energy and less money. It's pretty clear that utilizing indigenous materials in construction is a win-win: It allows us to save resources and can reduce initial capital investments.

Salvaging Tear-Down Components

We keep a lot of material out of landfills by handling teardowns efficiently. Our customers are also very excited about this value-added process; it allows them to participate with us in being socially and environmentally responsible, and it does not increase the costs of tearing down an older house or constructing a new infill home. In fact, our teardown practices have allowed us to turn what would have been disposal costs into income and have given us a competitive edge because potential clients like the opportunity to participate in waste reduction.

We deconstruct houses using conventional methods. We work with Eco-Recycle, a local waste diversion company, to sort and repurpose most of the materials. In a recent deconstruction, we were able to divert over 80% of the entire home a total of 233.8 tons diverted from just one house!

We are fortunate enough to have a relationship with Re-Source St. Louis, an entity that operates like to a co–op. Prior to dismantling a house, we can post components such as kitchen cabinets, fixtures, and other reusable items on Re-Source's Web site (www.resourcestlouis.org) so people can buy and reuse the materials. We also donate some of the viable components to organizations such as Habitat for Humanity or Homes, a non-profit organization that we formed to build green homes for injured and disabled veterans.

Another group, the Reuse People of America, a non-profit organization, comes to our homes to appraise various components. We then send them items they want, and our customers can claim a tax benefit. Then, Reuse People of America sells the items at a greatly reduced price compared with similar new items to areas that need the materials. This is a terrific solution for components from older homes that are no longer in style and are not in demand locally. These components still have great value in other areas including other countries.

In addition, we enjoy creatively handling teardown materials on-site. We might crush the old foundation, driveway, walkways, and other concrete components to use for fill under the new driveway. When you think about it, you can find plenty of ways to reuse materials for a new purpose.

Still toxic materials are a big challenge to recycling components from older teardowns. The good news is that the construction industry and innovative thinking health officials are constantly devising ingenious solutions for remediating and recovering such materials. Hopefully all of these hard-to-recycle items will find a new life in some form someday. Green builders, of course, advocate using only non-toxic materials in home construction. As others come on board and buy into green methods, the problem of how to dispose of toxic materials will eventually cease to exist.

Reusing Infrastructure by Building Infill Housing

Infill housing helps to spare woodlands, farms, park-lands, and rural areas from development, conserving crop-lands and preserving natural resources. It also helps to mitigate urban sprawl, makes use of existing urban amenities, and helps cities maintain a healthy tax base to support the many services they supply to their citizens. In short, infill housing recycles developed sites.

The most obvious advantage of infill housing is that the infrastructure already exists: streets, water, sewer, electricity, and transportation systems. Avoiding the expense of adding and maintaining new infrastructure represents good use of land, natural resources, and money.

All of this helps renew neighborhoods and create convivial communities in which people want to live. There are numerous advantages to infill housing:

- It maintains and increases property values.
- It can cut down on commute times, save gas, and decrease automotive pollution.
- It lessens highway congestion and reduces spending on new roads.
- It puts residents within easy reach of mass transit and the city's cultural attractions.

So why build anywhere else? Builders and developers are in business to build and develop. As with any business, your costs dictate how you carry out your mission. In the St. Louis area there is a large urban core that is growing, with many surrounding communities that are also growing. Sounds like anywhere USA, doesn't it?

For the past few years, it seemed a builder's biggest problem was keeping up with the demand for housing. Only a few years ago, our largest concern was having enough lots or land so we could keep up with demand and stay in business. In most municipalities in our metropolitan area, projects could take one to three years or longer to move through the approval process. The engineers who performed the design work merely created a plan that they felt confident would get through that onerous process with a number of lots that made the investment and delay still worthwhile.

When choosing where to develop based on time-lines for approvals, which areas would you develop in?

If you answered the ones with the most streamlined approval process, you would be like most builders and developers! Unfortunately, many of these areas are in outlying communities that have been criticized for promoting urban sprawl. However, some developers and builders that invested in the inner suburban areas got stuck with inventory when the housing market downturn began reducing overall property values.

Some areas, like the City of St. Louis, have revamped their approval process and streamlined approvals and even requested feedback from builders on how to handle green building. As a result, the city's population has grown for the first time in more than 40 years. Other areas have instituted what is referred to as *green taping* (as opposed to red taping), which expedites approval for green buildings. When government and industry work together, good things can happen!

There are always exceptions, of course. Sometimes existing infrastructure is too obsolete or there may be some other external obsolescence that hinders redevelopment, but the worthy concept and proven track record are too strong to deny.

CHAPTER 4

REDUCING ENERGY CONSUMPTION

M ost older traditional homes function as energy sieves, yet most home owners are unaware of how much energy their home and appliances needlessly waste each day. Wasting energy is like burning money! According to the Energy Information Administration, the typical U.S. family spends about $1,500 a year on utilities, only to have most of the energy escape through drafty doors, leaky windows, and poorly insulated walls. However, as energy prices continue to rise, home buyers are beginning to change their attitudes and are demanding energy-efficient homes. Savvy home buyers realize that an energy-efficient home not only costs less to operate and maintain, it is more comfortable and livable as well.

Energy efficiency encompasses not only a home's energy consumption, but also the energy required to build the house—from mining, manufacturing, and shipping to the building process itself. At every phase, green builders are interested in promoting efficient use of resources.

The Green Building Envelope

The Green Home Builder: Navigating for Success in a Down Economy report also found that by far, the most highly used green building feature is air tight sealing and construction and insulation of the building envelope. The *building envelope* consists of the floor, walls, windows, doors, and roof. The traditional envelope keeps out the elements, noise, dirt, and pests, and lets in natural light. Unfortunately, it also can leak a lot of energy.

By contrast, the *green envelope* offers all the benefits of the traditional building envelope, plus it is energy efficient. The green envelope incorporates superior insulating techniques and passive control functions that promote energy efficiency. The green envelope allows home buyers to live more comfortably and spend less on utilities.

My friend Peter Pfeiffer, a renowned green architect in Austin, Texas, puts it this way: "Think about the envelope of a building like your coat. To make it work better, button it up." And he's right. With the advances in building science, green builders can "build it tight and ventilate it right."

When I was working as a building codes official in the 1980s, after our last energy crisis, the building codes required that homes be built tighter. However, apparently, those who wrote the codes forgot that real people lived, cooked, showered, exercised, and breathed inside those tighter houses that trapped moisture and, in some cases, allowed mold to thrive. In addition, the prevalent materials of the 1980s and '90s off-gassed, filling some homes with toxic fumes that couldn't easily escape due to the tighter envelope. Materials such as traditional paints and flooring, which were used throughout the homes back then, contributed to the problem. Many of those dwellings are still occupied, of course, and will remain so for years to come.

Green building techniques allow builders to design toxicity out of housing by utilizing low-volatile organic compounds (VOCs) and nontoxic materials and finishes to minimize off-gassing, constructing tighter envelopes, an installing proper air-filtration systems and heat-recovery (or energy recovery) ventilators to help purify the air.

Windows

In the 1970s, as energy costs dramatically increased, researchers looked for ways to conserve energy and improve window performance. One answer was the double-pane window with air trapped between the panes. Air has about 10 times the heat resistance value of glass alone, so by simply including a space for air, window performance improved significantly. Additional experiments using alternative gases between the panes of glass led to using argon between the panes. Argon is a natural gas that is denser than air so it increases the insulating performance of the window even more.

In addition to using air or argon, adding selective coating and glazing to windows can greatly improve their performance. A thin coating on one of the inside panes of glass can increase the amount of radiated or sunlight energy transferred, or *emissivity*, through the window. The less radiant energy is transferred through the glass, the lower the emissivity, thus the term *Low-E*. The exterior pane of glass is sealed to keep cold out and prevent the window from fogging with condensation.

Another critical consideration when incorporating high performance windows is the amount of glass used in the home. Excessive amounts of glass can compromise the energy saving performance of the home. The high performance factor of the window allows their incorporation in the envelope—too much glass area will lessen overall performance.

Walls

In erecting walls, the primary objective is to create a high-performance wall that effectively copes with environmental conditions. To understand what that means, you need to know a basic thermodynamic principle: warm air and water will always try to move to cold air or water and will lose energy as they cool (or require more energy to stay warm). Wet air will move toward a dry area, where it will eventually evaporate (unless it is trapped inside a wall where it may stay wet and promote mold growth). Given these immutable laws, builders must construct walls in particular ways and use specific materials to ensure that they will keep a home cozy, comfortable, and healthy.

Foundation Walls

In areas that have full foundations, poured concrete foundations are the norm. This usually includes digging and setting footing forms, and then pouring the footings and setting wall forms made of wood and steel or aluminum. These forms are then filled with concrete. The last step is key: To ensure a strong foundation, builders must pay particular attention to the quality of the concrete and its placement on the jobsite. The travel time from the plant where the batch was mixed to the jobsite, and the temperature affect the amount of moisture in the mix. Adding too much water to the mixture at the jobsite to compensate for water evaporation while the concrete was in transit can weaken the material. Instead of water, adding *fly ash*, an inexpensive byproduct of coal-fired power plants, is becoming more common. This practice reduces the amount of materials that need to be mined to make a good batch of concrete.

Some newer building systems allow for an insulating material to be installed inside the forms as they are set and incorporated into the poured concrete wall to increase the insulating R-value. This technique requires a little more labor, however, because the form ties have to be routed through the material.

Another way to increase the insulating value of poured walls is to incorporate a premanufactured foam insulating sheathing system. It can be applied on the interior, or in some cases on the exterior, of the poured concrete wall. The edges of these foam sheets have tongue-and-groove fittings so they will close tightly to reduce air leakage. They attach to the foundation wall with mechanical fasteners.

No matter which system is used, the exterior of a poured concrete wall system requires application of a water-resistant treatment. This treatment is often a petroleum-based product which is sprayed on. In the cases where we use this system, the sprayed mixture we use contains recycled roof shingles. Another waterproofing method is a *foundation wrap*. This prefabricated membrane is designed to control groundwater around the foundation while allowing air to flow against the concrete to keep the foundation dry.

An optional improved foundation method we offer is an insulated precast foundation system. The foundation wall panels are precast with 5,000 psi normal weight concrete that incorporates synthetic fibers in a controlled manufacturing environment (fig. 15). These panels are delivered to the jobsite and erected using a crane. The panels are framed and preinsulated with polystyrene foam to meet **ENERGY STAR** requirements and can be readily finished without additional framing in the basement. The panels are cast in a manner that does not require additional waterproofing, thereby eliminating the need for the purchase,

Figure 15. Foundation wall panels

These walls can also be stacked and used in above ground wall applications where they offer durability and fire-resistance.

transport, and use of waterproofing materials. The panels are protected by a 15-year warranty against material and workmanship defects and sidewall groundwater penetration. These wall systems also do not require a poured concrete footing. Instead, they sit on a compacted ½ in. clean crushed-rock footing. They are engineered so the loads they carry do not require a spread concrete footing. They distribute the load to the soil underneath through the compacted crushed stone. Normal drain tile is installed to control groundwater penetration.

This system saves a step by eliminating the forming and pouring of a concrete spread footing. Moreover, walls can be set in colder temperatures that would hinder the pouring of concrete. Casting in a controlled environment improves the quality and consistency of the concrete throughout the wall. The system eliminates the need to add water onsite and have various loads of concrete with different slumps delivered. The finished wall is free of seams or honeycombs.

Crawlspaces

By using the proper techniques, such as a poured 2-in. minimum concrete slab floor in the crawlspace, builders can actually condition crawlspaces to control humidity and temperature, thereby enhancing building performance. Although it costs more, it helps control moisture, facilitates better air quality, and limits insect and rodent infestation. We have found that it makes our passive radon mitigation system more effective by eliminating the need to line the crawlspace with a heavy mil plastic, which is very difficult to do in a confined area like a crawlspace and on a bed of dirt and crushed rock.

Insulation

When building stick-frame construction, we insulate with fiberglass batts, spray cellulose, or nontoxic foams to fill the wall cavity to capacity to ensure maximum performance. Typical stick-frame construction results in an energy rating of about R-13 for 2×4 exterior walls and up to R-19 for 2×6 walls. We can also enhance insulation by sealing the wall-frame assembly (wall panels) to the floor and at panel intersections or installing exterior continuous foam sheathing underneath siding.

Fiberglass Batts

Fiberglass batts are the most popular type of insulation. This application is cost effective and fiberglass, as with most materials, performs very well when properly installed. All corners must be "tucked in" and wall cavities must be full. When using blown-in fiberglass in ceiling areas, you must verify that there are no voids and the insulation is of the proper depth. Manufacturers even provide wall insulation with built-in vapor control in the form of Kraft paper facing. In any case, you should always specify nonformaldehyde fiberglass.

Spray Cellulose

Spray cellulose is another cost-effective material. We use this type of insulation more than other. Most spray cellulose is made with recycled materials and contains a borate solution, which makes it insect and fire resistant. However, when choosing the specific product, you should pick one that contains a binder to prevent it from settling in the walls over time. It is sprayed in wet so we allow a day for drying before testing with a handheld moisture meter and encapsulating it with drywall. We refrain from using spray cellulose in attics because the amount of moisture used to spray it with adds more weight on top of the drywall ceiling than other types of insulation.

Spray Foam

Spray foam insulation comes in two basic types: *open cell* and *closed cell.* Open-cell foam is lighter and cheaper than closed cell. It also is less brittle, which allows it to flex inside walls as the building expands and contracts. When the tiny foam cells open, they allow in air, which is a good insulator. Open-cell insulation is less dense; however, and it has a slightly lower R-value.

Closed-cell foam is a durable product that captures the denser gas that is used to spray it with so that it expands inside the cells. As with the argon gas in the double-paned windows, this gas is a better insulator than air. However, it costs more and only provides a slight increase in R-value. You may be already using closed-cell products in your homes as some decorative trim pieces are made with closed-cell foam.

Again, proper installation is key to achieving the desired results. Both products are sprayed into the wall cavities and generally look like paint as they are applied. They expand very rapidly to fill openings and harden quickly so excess can be cut or scraped away. But if the applicator is not diligent, the product can expand so rapidly it actually pulls away from the exterior sheathing, leaving a void behind it that could trap and hold moisture.

Structural Insulated Panels

Using structural insulated panels (SIPs) we can build homes that are better insulated and more structurally sound. The SIP system offers a superior energy rating of R-25 for walls and R-45 for roof panels. SIPs replace the separate stick-framing, sheathing, and insulation components with an integrated system that is very tight and durable (fig. 16).

Proper insulation installation is as important as any other part of the home. Many years ago, when I was still "wet behind the ears," an old construction superintendant (at least at the time he seemed old) told me; "You don't get what you expect, you get what you inspect!" Truer words could not apply to the construction and insulation of a home!

The SIPs we use are manufactured in two phases. First, the polystyrene foam is manufactured and cut into sheets. Then, the structural elements, studs and/or engineered lumber, are incorporated. Oriented Strand Board (OSB), engineered plywood sheathing, is applied to both sides. This process creates a sturdy panel with few, if any, thermal breaks compared with a typical framed construction with studs. A heated

Figure 16. Side view of SIPs

This side view of a SIP shows how the panels form an integrated system of framing, sheathing, and insulation.

rod is used to burn electrical raceways vertically and horizontally through the panels, then switch and outlet locations are cut into the panels at predetermined locations. Additional switches and outlets can be easily added later.

We keep the majority of switchboxes and other electrical gear on interior walls to eliminate the need to provide electrical runs in the SIPS panels. Our SIPs do not have formaldehyde added to the foam. There is very little waste generated from the manufacture and use of SIPs. Excess foam from SIPs production is recycled by the manufacturer and other than wall bracing, there is very little cutting needed on the jobsite, which also saves time.

Wraps

Incorporating a high performance building wrap, such as Tyvek®, into the home design can also improve wall performance. Although it provides a general moisture barrier, building wrap is not a vapor barrier; therefore, it works to help slow heat transfer while allowing the home to breathe.

Wall systems such as SIPs might require a different building wrap from a conventionally framed wall. Typically the *permeance,* or *perm* rating, of the building wrap needed for a conventionally framed wall might be 12. However, because of the denser design and assembly of SIP walls a wrap that has a perm rating of 6 or lower, depending on the manufacturer's specifications, will work as well, because the walls are denser to begin with than in conventionally framed construction.

Different wall assemblies require different methods to control air and water vapor. You should research the manufacturer's requirements for controlling air and moisture flow with any type of wall system. This is as essential as properly constructing the wall. Familiarize yourself not only with how the walls are constructed and assembled but the appropriate types of insulation, vapor barrier, building wrap, and sealing and flashing systems that will ensure those wall systems perform properly.

> We've all heard the saying, "Build it tight and ventilate it right." I'd like to add, " If you build it tight, you'd best build it right!"

Air-Sealing Package

To make the building envelope most efficient, we need to button it up, that is, to seal the small air leaks that are inevitable in construction. At Belcher Homes, when we assemble a home from its components, we focus on creating a good airtight fit (figs. 17, 18). We realize that there will be small air gaps, so we seal those gaps with a quality, nontoxic caulk or foam compound. A number of manufacturers produce nontoxic, low-VOC sealing materials.

Figure 17. Sealing floor joists

Gaps usually occur at joins, where the floor plate and walls meet, or where two walls meet.

Figure 18. Sealing rim joists

Sealing along plate lines and wall intersection, around rim joists, etc. Using low-VOC caulks is easy to do and enhances overall wall performance dramatically.

Gaps also occur around doors, windows, switchboxes, and outlets. These areas can be the source of significant air leaks, so they should be sealed to maintain the R-value of the insulation and performance of the wall itself. After we have sealed all gaps, we perform a thorough visual inspection and run a blower-door test to verify the integrity of the building envelope, which will reveal any unsealed gaps.

Windows and Doors

As discussed previously, better performing windows manufactured using insulated glass with Low-E coating slow heat and energy transfer. Thermal windows, which contain an argon gas sandwiched between their glass panels, and similarly constructed insulated doors, are very durable and typically last 20 or more years.

ENERGY STAR-rated windows are tested and rated to prove that they window allow less heat (energy) to transfer through the window frame and glazing.

Even the construction of window components have become greener. For example, window manufacturers are producing windows with certified sustainable wood. The windows are clad with a durable material such as vinyl or metal to protect the wood from the elements and enhance insulating performance and durability (fig. 19). At the end of its useful life, the entire window is recyclable.

Notice that the window shown in Figure 20 qualifies as ENERGY STAR only in specific regions of the country, as the label indicates. In the climate zone that includes the St. Louis area, for example, the energy code currently requires a minimum *U-factor*, a measure of heat flow, of 0.49. (The window's energy performance rating includes both the U-factor and *R-value*, or resistance to heat flow.) The lower the U-factor, the less heat moves through the window. In northern states like Minnesota, the U-factor is 0.31, which would require a different window that what

Figure 19. Window cross section

When windows are constructed in this fashion they comply with and are able to carry the ENERGY STAR-rating.

qualifies as ENERGY STAR in our area. The *solar heat gain coefficient* is the amount of solar heat gain that passes or "radiates" though the window (in this example 0.30 equals 33%). *Visible transmittance* is basically the amount of light transmitted. This usually is not as large a factor with residential construction as it is with commercial applications.

Nontoxic sealants around windows and doors on the interior, durable caulk around the exterior, and

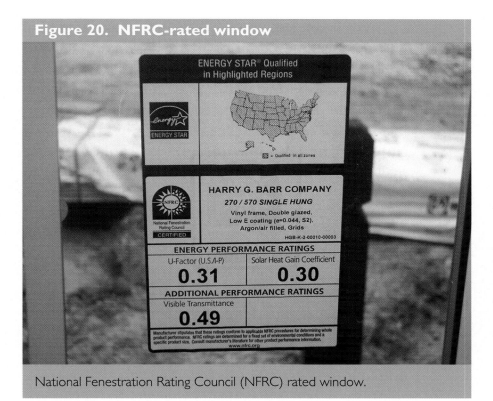

Figure 20. NFRC-rated window

National Fenestration Rating Council (NFRC) rated window.

foam insulation in door jambs tightens the envelope, preventing air leaks and reducing heat transfer.

Well-insulated doors are usually made of fiberglass or insulated steel. Both of these materials are completely recyclable. Like windows, doors are basically a hole in a well-insulated wall or the weak link in the building envelope. Understanding how window and door openings can compromise the envelope you so carefully constructed with the walls is key to minimizing energy loss.

A well-insulated door, whether it is insulated steel with an insulated core or fiberglass manufactured and finished to look like wood, is only as good as its application and installation. A home's design positively influences a door's performance when the design incorporates features such as a breezeway, a mudroom (interior room), or at a minimum, a roof or awning over the exterior door, to protect the door and to separate it from the main living areas. Of course, these design conditions are not always present. In those cases, the door's construction is imperative. A good quality door is useless if the jamb and frame assembly are substandard (fig. 21).

Composite materials increase door functionality and durability, and extend the life of the unit as a whole. Also, sill flashing to prevent intrusion below the door sill and other new flashing products are available to match siding colors. These are inexpensive solutions, when you consider the benefit they offer.

Roof Trusses

Usually a roof truss top cord sits on the plate of the wall; this reduces the clearance between top and bottom cord and will compress the insulation in that area (fig. 22). It may seem inconsequential, until you consider how many roof trusses there are in a house. Having uncompressed insulation at every point in the attic and roof area enhances energy efficiency and eliminates weak links in the home's thermal envelope.

Figure 21. Door frame

Many manufacturers use soft wood exterior door units, jambs, and molding, which despite aggressive maintenance, still degrade within a few years and have to be replaced.

Figure 22. Roof truss energy heel detail

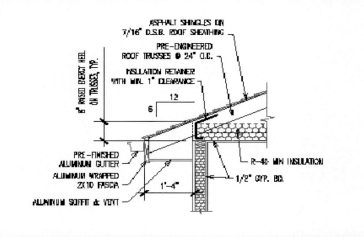

We use a raised energy heel on trusses to raise the stand of the top cord, a technique that prevents compression.

Roof

For homes we build with conventional roofs, we offer home buyers the option of selecting Thermastrand™ roof sheathing. It has a foil-like surface that faces the attic area, insulating the attic from the radiant heat of the roof. It prevents the penetration of UV rays and keeps the roof and attic space cooler, so shingles last longer and the climate inside the home can be controlled more easily and efficiently. It is just another product we can offer to help a home perform better. Although it is not practical economically in all situations, it works well in most applications.

HVAC Design, Equipment, and Installation

If you pay attention to solar design, construct an airtight building envelope, and seal air leaks, chances are very good that you can downsize the HVAC equipment. Downsizing the HVAC system lowers the initial installation costs as well as future operating costs. Furthermore, because you have focused on constructing the envelope of the house to perform better overall, the HVAC system will run less often and more efficiently, lowering maintenance costs. This approach to HVAC system design applies to your traditional electric or gas unit with blower, a heat pump, or a geothermal unit. In any case, you should include a knowledgeable HVAC contractor on your team and have that person help you incorporate a pilot design before you deploy it widely.

To be knowledgeable, the HVAC contractor needs be abreast of current equipment as well as building techniques and building science. Sometimes it seems as though most HVAC systems are designed to compensate for a lack of planning the site and home design. Some systems are designed as though homes are located in areas where the sun shines on all four walls continuously during the summer and not at all in the winter. This approach may be effective to compensate for other shortcomings in the planning and construction process but it can be very inefficient and costly over a long period of time.

A good HVAC system includes three elements: HVAC and heat pump efficiency, geothermal design, and solar power.

HVAC and Heat Pump Efficiency

Traditionally, homes have been built with an electric or gas furnace and an air conditioner. Although high-efficiency versions of HVAC equipment have been on the market for decades, they have become more widespread only recently as the cost of energy increases.

When considering HVAC systems, builders should match the equipment to the type of home they are constructing and the climate of its location. For example, new requirements stipulate that air conditioners and heat pumps must meet a level 13 seasonal energy efficiency rating (SEER). We install a minimum of 14 SEER. Because we have more cooling days than heating days, on average, than the North, this rating is more important for us and for other builders in the South and the Midwest. In the North, heating efficiency is the primary HVAC concern; however, the dividing line for cooling days versus heating days is slowly creeping north. Whether you believe in global warming or consider warmer temperatures the result of some other trend, you need to consider whether heating or cooling is the primary concern in your geographic region.

Budget also may influence equipment selection. Although traditional HVAC units and heat pumps are somewhat less expensive to install than a geothermal unit, indoor temperature can vary by up to five degrees from the set point on the thermostat, even if you selected only one degree of variance. You can mitigate this effect somewhat by installing a high-efficiency HVAC unit with a higher price tag. This type of unit uses a variable speed fan to control temperature variance. The fan generally operates at a slower speed, which saves energy; however, it runs more frequently to circulate and distribute air and draws the air across the filter more often. It also can cycle at a higher speed as needed.

Geothermal Design

New federal tax incentives are making geothermal very affordable. Several states are adding further incentives for solar, wind, and geothermal. With today's technology, geothermal is more efficient in residential applications than solar and wind combined, especially in areas further north.

The geothermal system uses a loop to circulate water for heating or cooling, taking advantage of the Earth's consistent temperature of 56 degrees. A horizontal loop installed at a depth of about 10 ft. (depending on soil conditions) is the most efficient method. However, due to space constraints most systems are installed in "drilled" holes at a depth of 150 ft. because you need approximately 300 ft. of "loop" per ton of heating and cooling in this type of installation (figs. 23, 24).

Therefore, after water flows through the coils and returns to the HVAC unit, its temperature is 56 degrees. The furnace heats from this baseline, while the air conditioner merely circulates the air—with no compressor required and dumps the removed heat into the ground to dissipate. The system fan runs at a slow speed, but for a longer period, which adds to the comfort level inside the home as air is drawn

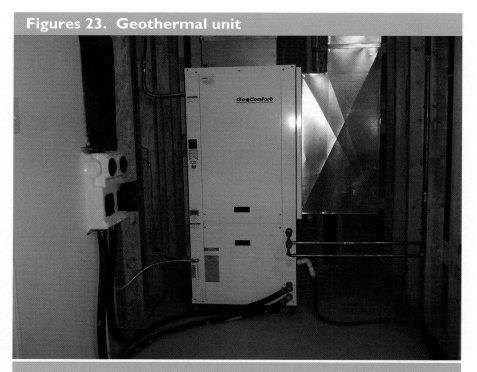

Figures 23. Geothermal unit

A geothermal system, which uses the ground as a heat exchanger, is much more efficient than a traditional HVAC unit or heat pump.

Figures 24. Geothermal drilling

Due to space constraints many geothermal systems in new and existing construction are installed in boreholes. We typically protect our systems by installing them under driveways. Once they are installed, no future maintenance should be needed for the piping.

across the filters more often. Once installed this unit provides all of the heating, cooling, and preheated water to the water heater, which leads to a savings in utility bills for home buyers.

We also work with our HVAC design team and advise our clients about the practicality of installing an energy recovery ventilator (ERV), often also referred to as a *heat recovery ventilator* or (HRV). It is simply a heat exchanger installed to capture some of the heated air in a home and use it to pre-warm incoming fresh air to reduce the energy (and cost) needed to heat it from ambient.

We've had to adapt commercial ERV or HRV units to fit the homes we built. Today, manufacturers are incorporating new materials, finishes, and ventilation systems, and producing new filters and recovery ventilation systems specifically for residential application. These new systems are not only more cost effective, they also can help improve air quality inside older homes at a more reasonable cost. Simply stated, ERV and HRV make the building systems perform better.

Solar Power

The cost and reliability of traditional sources of energy have increased consumer focus on and interest in solar power. Almost all potential clients we meet ask about incorporating solar power into their homes. During the past few years, we have had thunderstorms and ice storms in our area that left a large number of homes without power for an extended period of time during very hot and very cold weather. These events have spurred more clients to inquire about adding solar power to their homes. Because installing solar power in homes is still expensive compared with other types of installations ($20,000 to $25,000 for a complete system), we prewire homes to receive solar power in the future as the price of the technology comes down.

We install a combiner box in an attic or upper floor area and run a cable to a disconnect box near the electric panel in the lower level. The owners can easily install one to eight strands of photovoltaic or improved solar technology in a few years when the price comes down, the technology advances, and energy prices are the same or higher than they are today (fig. 2). They can take some equity in their home and reinvest it in something that will most likely make them a very good return on the investment.

If you decide to take this approach to offering a solar technology option, make sure the home you are building or retrofitting will not be shaded by a taller home or other obstacle to sunlight in the future.

An increasing array of incentives is being offered for home owners to incorporate active solar design. For example, prior to 2007 Missouri had a net metering law that required a utility company to buy excess power generated by these systems. However, because the rules were vague, utilities bought the power at the nominal off-peak rate.

However, two years ago the law was changed to specify buyback rates would reflect actual market prices. In addition, the federal government offers several initiatives to provide tax credits for incorporating alternative energy into building design. These incentives, combined with the increasing affordability of solar technology and rising utility prices in general, are making active solar increasingly feasible.

The appearance of solar installations has improved greatly from the panels of the early 1970s. They are much less obtrusive. We build homes in many rural areas and even if those clients do not like the appearance of photovoltaics on their roofs, they can place the solar equipment on a barn roof, trellis, or other ancillary structure.

Water Heating Design

An efficient water heating design is a win-win for the builder and the home owner. It decreases the amount of energy lost in transit because the hot water does not have to travel too far. As a result, the home owner's operating costs are lower. Because this method of design requires less piping and installation labor, the builder's initial construction costs are lower as well.

Belcher Homes designs houses so that water can be efficiently heated and distributed. Showers account for approximately 18% of indoor water use and sinks for about 15%. Efficient design can substantially reduce the quantity of water used each month in both of these applications, thereby lowering the home owner's utility bills.

One method that Belcher Homes uses in efficient design is to centralize the location of the water heater and then cluster or align the bathrooms and the kitchen. Laundering clothes accounts for approximately 23% of indoor water use each month and because most people use warm or hot water washing cycles, it pays to also place the washing machine as close to the water heater as possible.

Our design approach also requires that we insulate hot and cold water pipes. This helps conserve water, because the home owner does not have to run gallons of water, for example, to achieve the desired shower temperature. Depending on the home buyer's budget, we can install a pump with return piping to send unused hot water back to the water heater for even greater efficiency. We have switched to installing cross-linked polyethylene (PEX) piping systems. This tubing can be threaded, like wiring, throughout the household. PEX systems on average have about 90% fewer elbows than copper piping and use no chemicals for connections. The piping also is not as affected by freezing and thawing. Manufacturing PEX requires less energy and the product is recyclable. One has to be vigilant in installing these systems, however, so tubing does not rest against abrasive or sharp edges, such as joist hangers, because the vibration from water flow will cause the tubing to wear if it rests against those materials.

We also insulate the standard tank water heater, which helps to conserve energy by keeping water temperature at the set point for a longer period of time. This means the heater fires up less frequently, which conserves energy and lowers utility bills. A more constant supply of hot water also makes the house more livable and comfortable. To improve indoor air quality, we can also install a power ventilator on the heater to control products of combustion and protect indoor air quality.

Tankless water heaters are very efficient, because they supply hot water quasi on-demand. However, the maintenance requirements, including regular flushing, can make them much costlier than a standard hot water tank. We build custom homes in areas where well water and/or hard water is common. In these cases, we strongly recommend using tankless heater specifically designed for hard water installations in conjunction with a water softener, which can extend the life of the heater and lower maintenance (or replacement) costs (fig. 3).

Belcher Homes also offers solar water heating, through innovative products such as Velux Corporation's solar water heating system. It is an easily installed system that can be tied into your new or existing water heater. With federal incentives, if these systems are SRCC certified, you could qualify for up to a 30% tax credit for installing these active solar devices.

Energy-Efficient Lighting and Appliances

New, energy-efficient lighting systems, fixtures and bulbs are emerging on the market in a big way, and green builders are using them, along with natural light, to make homes more comfortable, while decreasing the use of coal to generate electricity and other non-renewable fossil fuels.

Improved indoor lighting systems not only consume far less energy, they generate less heat as well, which reduces the strain on air-conditioning. They also cost less to maintain. Thanks to ever advancing technology, you can purchase and install many types of lighting for less today than you could have previously.

For example, green compact fluorescent light (CFL) bulbs are within reach for every home owner and builder. We should all take advantage of these energy-efficient bulbs; the energy they save helps to offset the 80+ million tons of mercury that coal-fired plants generate every year in producing electricity. But what, you might ask, about the small amount of mercury in a CFL bulb? It could easily and safely be recovered and recycled, but the collection of used bulbs will have to be simplified and made more convenient to encourage most people to participate in recycling their used CFL bulbs.

Since ENERGY STAR has reworked its requirements for labeling, you can be more confident in using labeled fixtures and bath exhaust fans. We work with a good lighting consultant to help advise our clients about their lighting selections. These professionals are familiar with our green building efforts and help our clients actually save money and time in making the proper lighting selections for the proper locations.

In terms of exterior lighting, we avoid *uplighting*—the use of spotlights to illuminate shrubbery, walls, and features on the exteriors, in order to comply with green *dark sky* guidelines, which are intended to reduce energy use and *light pollution*. Although uplighting can dramatically enhance a building's appearance at night, it does so at great cost. Besides the fact that it wastes enormous amounts of energy and money, it also is believed to disrupt bird migrations and definitely obscures the view of the night sky by fading out the number of visible stars.

In my opinion, uplighting diminishes the beauty of the natural world at night by screening it from our sight. If you had a choice, wouldn't you rather see the stars? I know I would.

As previously discussed, typical home construction today provides new homes that are 100% more energy efficient than homes constructed only 10 years ago. However, 97.5% of all homes are 10 or more years old. In the average American home, appliances consume about 40% of energy to power computer chips, clocks, and other standby devices even while they are turned off! This phenomenon is referred to as the *phantom load*.

In new construction, even though it is exponentially more energy efficient than older existing homes, energy demand by the occupants is the primary factor in energy consumption. As more and more appliances, entertainment devices, chargers for items such as cell phones (which typically consume about the same amount of electricity weather or not the phone or device is plugged into it) are being used, this energy use, often referred to as *plug load* in combination with older less energy efficient appliances compromises the gains made in the energy efficient construction of the home itself.

This is one reason why consumer education, which is discussed further in chapter 7, is so important. We hate to include cost efficient methods that lead to ongoing cost savings for the consumer, only for them to go out and spend that savings on more electronics that will compromise the efficiencies we designed and built into their homes.

ENERGY STAR-rated appliances reduce or eliminate some of this phantom load, thus lowering energy bills and slowing the need to construct new and ever-larger power plants. As with lighting, appliances continue to improve in energy efficiency. American manufacturers, such as Whirlpool, are following the lead of European manufacturers in creating energy-efficient product lines.

One appliance we offer is the ASKO dishwasher, which is extremely energy and water efficient. Every ASKO component in all of the company's appliances is tagged for recycling. And, ASKO discharges waste-water that is actually cleaner than the water piped into their plants! The ASKO manufacturing plant, including its environmental management, is now ISO-14001 certified. At ASKO, one good thing led to another. The company now runs more efficiently, and the benefits of its improved environmental management standards cascade into the world, touching the lives of others in positive ways. I think that such a green approach to appliance design and manufacturing is well worth emulating.

Since 1992, The U.S. Environmental Protection Agency (EPA) has set the criteria for ENERGY STAR ratings and works with hundreds of manufacturers to improve the energy efficiency of appliances. The special ENERGY STAR label is awarded only to the most energy-efficient appliances.

The ENERGY STAR for Homes program has been a partnership between the EPA and the U.S. Department of Energy (DOE) since 1996. In 2006, the penetration of ENERGY STAR Homes as a part of the market had reached 12%. Since 1996, that percentage of the new homes market has grown rapidly and with the expansion of green building programs around the country using ENERGY STAR as the focus of their energy requirements. The ENERGY STAR program has become the benchmark for energy-efficient construction in the housing industry.

Currently, ENERGY STAR appliances can reduce energy consumption by up to 30% on average, and manufacturers are working to increase that rate of efficiency. As more households acquire more of these appliances, the savings in energy and money will multiply dramatically. Belcher Homes only installs ENERGY STAR appliances in the homes we build.

Home Energy Rating Specialist (HERS)

A performance test by a Home Energy Rating Specialist (HERS) verifies the energy efficiency of a new or existing home. In essence, it details the home's current state of performance and explains if and where improvements are needed in order for it to be rated a high-performance home.

The performance test also shows exactly where a builder or home owner must fine-tune the building envelope and air-sealing package, for example, so there is no guesswork. The process is similar to building an engine: you build, test the energy efficiency, and then add high-performance parts as needed to increase power and performance.

Most HERS raters go through a formal training process prescribed by the Residential Energy Services Network (RESNET), the largest organization that develops criteria and procedures for HERS raters. The DOE and the EPA designated RESNET, its program, and verifiers for the ENERGY STAR program. The HERS rater is an important part of a green building or remodeling team. If a builder/remodeler involves the HERS rater in the design process and incorporates the rater's recommendations, and if the house performs to ENERGY STAR guidelines, then the builder and the house meet most of the green energy standards of NAHB, LEED-H, and local green building programs.

As part of performance testing, the HERS rater runs the following blower-door test:

1. The rater seals the house.
2. The rater installs a membrane with a fan in it over a door opening to exhaust the air out of the house, which creates negative air pressure in the house.
3. The rater uses smoke pencils to detect any air infiltration and its source and meters the pressure differential inside the house.
4. After the rater has noted any problem areas, the builder gathers the data to confirm the fresh air and comfort needs of the client.

In Missouri, state lawmakers passed tax-credit legislation to give existing home owners a credit to recover the cost associated with an energy evaluation of their older homes. The law includes a clause that requires home owners who undergo an audit to make improvements to enhance the energy efficiency of their home based on the audit's results. This is one example of how well-crafted tax-credit legislation can encourage more efficient use of natural resources. It will help push the energy efficiency of existing homes towards the levels achieved in new construction. It will also lead to more economic opportunity, as green remodelers are called upon to make these energy efficiency improvements.

For homes constructed using SIPs walls and a SIPs roof, the ENERGY STAR program requires only a visual inspection and completion of the visual inspection checklist, not a full performance test. However to ensure energy efficiency and verify performance of the home as a system and to make sure we have good baseline data, Belcher Homes performs a test on every house we build through a certified HERS rater. We check for proper air exchanges and excellent indoor air quality, among other things.

CHAPTER 5

CONSERVING WATER

One of the oldest points of development controversy in history is water. In Missouri, for example, we were arguing with states and communities upstream about their decision to dam the rivers more than a century ago. We have tremendous water resources in St. Louis—the Missouri, Mississippi, Illinois, and Meramec rivers, as well as many other abundant rivers, lakes, and streams. Water shortage has not been an issue yet. Still, as we consider seasonal water flows, rainfall, and increasing demand for water up and down our rivers, we realize must plan ahead and map out water allocation, including who gets what and when.

In some states, the water situation is already pretty dire. My friend Steve Hale, a home builder in New Mexico, where many naturally arid areas have been thirsting under a scorching eight-year drought, has had to make adjustments in order to build homes that use even less water. Steve and other builders within their local green building program, Build Green New Mexico, are on a quest to achieve super water efficiency. Their bone-dry environment and burgeoning populations don't leave them much choice.

We have reasonably priced technology to conserve water and to use it efficiently. When individuals and communities reduce their water usage, they lower their utility bills and usage and avoid the expenses of additional infrastructure construction and maintenance. Water savings are far-reaching and significant, involving water itself as well as everything involved in its collection, treatment, distribution, disposal, and cost. A lot needs to happen to water between the source and when it comes out of the faucet.

The world needs active hydrological reforms to mitigate looming water shortages and potentially more volatile climate changes. This is a prime example of how green building techniques offer practical solutions for the complex problems associated with water scarcity. Advances in plumbing, appliance functions, drainage, and landscaping can help home owners conserve water and save money while enjoying a livable, beautiful, and functionally efficient home.

Plumbing

Plumbing fixture technology has rapidly evolved, and major manufacturers are now producing fixtures to serve in line with new market standards. For example, before 1980, most toilets guzzled about five to six gallons per flush. By 1990, manufacturers were designing toilets that required only 3.5 gallons to do the job. Then, in 1992, Congress passed the Energy Policy Act, which stipulated that starting in 1994, toilets could use only 1.6 gallons of water, or less, per flush.

The first low-flow toilets were not well received by consumers, however, because they required more than one flush to clear the bowl, thereby negating any potential water savings. Now, new high-efficiency toilets use 20% less water per flush (an average of 1.3 gallons) than previous low-flow models and are winning rave reviews from customers because they clear the bowl in one flush. Some models still on the drawing board may even render flush toilets obsolete. Water-conserving toilets are only one part of an overall effort to reduce daily per-person water usage in single family homes, which is now 80 to 100 gallons, according to the U.S. Geological Survey. Sinks account for about 15% of indoor water use, showers about 18%, washing machines about 23%, and toilets about 26%.

Improved water efficiency leads to overall energy efficiency, because reducing water use in bathrooms, kitchens, laundry rooms, and elsewhere in the home, reduces the energy water treatment plants need to purify drinking water and the energy sewage treatment plants to treat wastewater. Water conservation, an important part of NAHB's Green Building Program, will have a global impact.

In addition to better plumbing fixtures, better water heating and distribution design can help significantly reduce water and energy use. This approach, coupled with more water-efficient plumbing fixtures such as low-flow toilets and showerheads, can lessen our impact on water and energy resources and save money for everyone.

We have the plumbing technology to help us move forward in a sustainable manner. We know how to make dramatic improvements in household water efficiency while maintaining a comfortable lifestyle and sustaining our shared water resources. As a green builder, I see an increasing interest among home owners in making smarter use of water.

Our water resources are finite, and our generation holds the key to the future—will we bequeath enough water and better water-conservation practices to future generations, or will they inherit drought, hardpan, and depleted resources? Will the availability and affordability of water lead to relocation of population?

Water-Efficient Appliances

Laundering clothes accounts for approximately 23% of indoor water use in U.S. homes. This is largely because of the prevalence of vertical-axis washing machines. Most Americans rely on these top-loading washing machines to clean their clothes. These washers agitate laundry in a big tub of water, a method that often tangles the items and requires relatively long spin cycles to then wring them out. The washer does not handle bulky items particularly well, either, with the agitator in the center of the tub.

There is another more efficient option. If you have ever used a Laundromat, then you have probably encountered horizontal-axis washing machines— front-loading washers that have no central agitator. You load clothes through a door on the front of the machine into a drum that rotates during wash and rinse cycles. This washer uses 40 to 75% less water than top-loading models and requires less detergent. It subjects clothes to less wear and tear, because they are not agitated, and it virtually eliminates tangling. The drum construction provides more space for bulky items such as mattress pads, down comforters, and heavy bedspreads.

Beyond using less water and soap, front-loading washers do not require as much time to complete a wash cycle; therefore, they use less energy. As for the clean factor, many people maintain that front-loading washers do a better job of cleaning clothes than top-loading models. To realize substantial water, energy and time savings, use a front-loading washing machine in conjunction with one of the new energy-efficient clothes dryers. These dryers work faster and use less heat.

Although dishwashing accounts for only 1% of indoor water use, new energy-efficient dishwashers still can save water and energy while cleaning dishes better than ever. Some dishwashers can even adjust water usage depending on how soiled the dishes are. Others now contain their own water heaters, so they need only a cold-water line. Most require less dishwashing detergent and work well with new enzyme-based cleaning agents.

There are even small countertop dishwashers that require no electricity; the line pressure of hot water from the kitchen sink faucet drives the cleaning cycle. Ultrasonic dishwashers are now beginning to appear on the market as well, offering ultra-efficient water and energy use and promising cleaner dishes in less time.

Rainwater Collection Systems

Each time it rains, free water flows off roofs, pavement, and other impervious surfaces. In most cases, it flows into gutters, which guide it into storm sewers, or it is absorbed by lawns and gardens. But what if you could harvest much of that rainwater and store it for later use?

Harvesting rainwater used to be a common practice in U.S. households, and it remains so in many countries. After all, rainwater-holding cisterns have been in use for thousands of years, as archeological excavations have shown. This ancient and sensible idea is once again becoming popular, as more people begin to understand the value of all this free water. This green approach to obtaining water eventually could become part of the daily water source for houses.

When Belcher Homes builds a house, we can install barrels at the bottom of downspouts or install a modern version of the underground cistern for water storage. For example, we design rainwater-collection methods to supply water for use in gardens and to slow storm water runoff. In the Midwest, spring rains alone will supply enough stored water to last until at least mid-summer for watering lawns and native plants in gardens (fig. 25).

Rain gardens are another green method for collecting and managing rainwater. Belcher Homes creates rain gardens by grading small bioretention areas around a site to slow down the water without completely stopping it. These slightly sunken areas of the lawn form low spots where rainwater will settle and slowly percolate into the ground. In our rain gardens, we plant native species suitable for such a niche ecosystem. Together, the ground and the native

Figure 25. Rain barrel

My clients, the Pedersens, installed rain barrels at each of their downspout locations. They landscaped their home with native plants so their need for irrigation is limited and the rain barrels provide plenty of water with which to do so.

plants can absorb rainwater in about 72 hours, which slows runoff, and filters the water as it is absorbed. Mosquitoes are not a problem, because many decorative native plant species attract mosquito-eating birds and insects, such as dragonflies, which help control the mosquito population.

In larger developments, we design the rain gardens of each individual home site to function as an integrated part of the storm water treatment chain for the entire locale. Our LID plan calls for this type of grand-scale implementation, because we feel a comprehensive approach to storm water management will create a beautiful, livable neighborhood that is also ecofriendly.

A key for builders and buyers alike: You should define maintenance criteria that protect the rain gardens in your entire development by subdivision indenture or by deed restriction. This ensures that the rain gardens will be maintained, thrive, and can continue to do their job properly. Moreover, as part of home owner education that national green building and development programs require, home owners should be educated about the proper types of pesticides and herbicides to use that will not harm the rain garden's high performance ecosystem.

For just a moment, envision a storm water recovery system made up of rain gardens, bioswales, and underground cisterns. Imagine rainwater percolating down into the cisterns, filtered by native plants and the ground. Why couldn't that clean, stored water supply nonpotable needs like irrigation, cooling, and even toilet flushing? Why not take advantage of free, off-the-grid water when good old Mother Nature offers it to us? It is happening now and coming to a new community near you!

CHAPTER 6

CONSTRUCTING A HEALTHY HOUSE

Some older traditional homes could literally make their owners sick due to poor air quality, excessive moisture, and pollutants generated in the home. Green homes, by contrast, are all about creating a healthy indoor environment.

Who wants to live in a house that is inefficient, high-maintenance, poorly insulated, and drafty? Who wants to breathe in formaldehyde from cabinets and toxic fumes from carpets and flooring? Do home owners really want to inhale chlorine mist in the shower? Green office buildings that promote healthier work environments have proliferated rapidly; it is equally important for workers to live in healthy homes. By reduc-

Building green is more than just designing the right conditions for good indoor air quality. It's about creating a healthy home environment.

ing potential indoor sources of pollutants and improving ventilation, green construction can enhance the livability and sustainability of the home.

Minimizing Potential Sources of Pollutants

Building a healthy house doesn't just start at the interior finish stage; it begins with protecting the materials builders order for every component in the house. Even rough framing lumber, including engineered lumber, is now fabricated using nontoxic glues and epoxies. Moreover, it includes very low or no urea-formaldehyde content. As soon as materials arrive at the jobsite, they should be covered with tarps (figs. 26, 27).

A few years ago we had a load of subflooring lumber delivered on a Friday for an installation that was to begin on the following Monday morning. Even though the weather forecast was for a clear weekend, I decided to throw some tarps over the lumber. Sure enough, Mother Nature threw us a curve ball, and on Saturday we had some light freezing rain.

On Sunday, my customers paid a surprise visit to the jobsite, as many home buyers do, to keep tabs on what is happening with their house when it is under construction. They called to thank me for

Figure 26. Tarped subfloor

A tarped subfloor lumber load just after delivery. We cover the lumber loads when delivered and overnight to reduce exposure to rain and snow. It also deters theft as it takes and extra effort to untarp prior to stealing!

caring enough about their house to tarp their lumber. So, my gut instinct about protecting the lumber paid two immediate dividends:

1. Moisture was kept out of the wood.
2. My customers were impressed with the high quality of Belcher Homes' construction methods.

Figure 27. Tarped SIPs

A stack of panelized construction components—in this case, SIPs—on the jobsite. As with all other materials, we use tarps to help minimize contamination and moisture damage.

Of course, there is no way to keep all moisture or dirt out of a house under construction. However, builders can benefit in the long run if they take steps to limit the exposure of materials to moisture, dirt, and other contaminants.

This underscores an advantage of panelized construction (fig. 28). Because the house is covered so much faster than with traditional stick-framing, builders not only will save time and reduce jobsite waste, they can build a cleaner, drier home right

Figure 28. Sample spec sheet

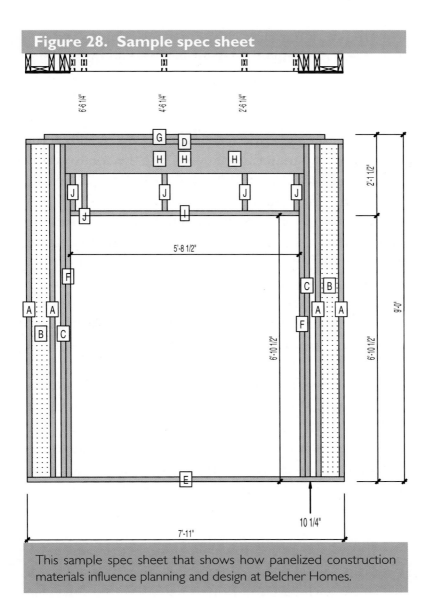

This sample spec sheet that shows how panelized construction materials influence planning and design at Belcher Homes.

from the start. Panelized building components are produced in a controlled environment and go up rapidly.

Once we reach the interior finish stage, we continue to specify components that are nontoxic and
contain low or no VOC—paints, glues, caulks, sealants,
flooring and casework, for example. We research the
MSDS for each material that goes into the construction
of the house to ensure that our customers will be safe
in their future home.

When my company installs fuel-fired equipment,
such as HVAC systems, water heaters, and fireplaces
we select only power-vented equipment and direct-
vent it to the outside. This reduces the risk of carbon
monoxide gases and other byproducts of combustion accumulating in the air inside the home and
affecting indoor air quality and endangering the
occupants.

Garages can be a significant source of pollutants
in the home. When we design a house, therefore, we
prefer to build detached garages, if possible. If the
house plans call for an attached garage, we install a
continuous air barrier between the garage and the
house, using building wrap or another type of vapor
barrier, as well as a gasketed door to prevent garage
fumes from entering the house.

If the lot layout allows, we design the house with
the garage located on the north or northwest side of
the house, so it can function as a windbreak. This also
helps to shield the house from windblown dirt and
other contaminants.

Managing Potential Pollutants Generated in the Home

To construct a green home, builders must consider every system within it, understand how those systems can generate pollutants, and then design the home to create a healthy indoor environment. Belcher Homes employs some practical yet very effective techniques to manage potential pollutants.

HVAC and Filters

During construction, we cover all HVAC-supply registers and grills to keep out dust and construction debris. After the house is complete, we vacuum the registers and grills again as part of our final cleaning process. It is very important to us that our customers enter a spotless, new green home—including clean HVAC ductwork. This attention to detail set us apart from our competitors.

As part of incorporating a high-efficiency heating system into a home, we install filters that have a higher minimum efficiency reporting value (MERV) rating and a variable-speed fan. One result is that air moves over the filter more often, improving indoor air quality without compromising energy efficiency. We add humidifiers and dehumidifiers to the HVAC system, depending on location and climate conditions. Where there is high humidity, for example, the moisture-laden air is a good carrier for mold and other pollutants. Controlling humidity levels in a house allows the home owner to raise the air-conditioning set point and lower the heating set point by several degrees, yet maintain a home that feels comfortable.

The proper use of the HVAC system and its filters are one of the best methods to maintaining air quality. Although there are several types of aftermarket air cleaners, few are practical. Those based on using ozone, for example, can actually be detrimental to the fit and finishes of the home. Whereas ozone in the atmosphere protects us from the sun, at ground level, it is harsh on paint finishes and plastics.

Venting

All exhaust—bath, kitchen range exhaust fan, fireplace, flues from the furnace, and hot water heater, for example—must be completely vented to the outside. If you build homes that have fireplaces or fuel-burning appliances, be sure there is an adequate supply of combustion and ventilation air to minimize the chance of backdrafting, which presents a carbon monoxide hazard.

Canopy-style kitchen hood fans can operate at 500 to 600 CFM or much higher. They are so powerful they can draw heating and cooling from the interior of the house to the outside. Plus, such fans can create a dangerous backdraft situation. If you build homes that include this type of hood fan on the kitchen range, I recommend that you install an intake fan to provide makeup air. Depending on the power of the fan, you might also have to temper (heat) the exhaust air so greases do not coagulate in the vent system as it is fanned by the cooler air from inside the home that is being exhausted. Alternatively, you could opt to install a smaller fan that is appropriately sized for home use.

Fans in the bath and laundry are supposed to exhaust moisture-laden air to the outside, so it does not collect in these rooms and promote the growth of mold and mildew. To be sure the fan stays on long enough to perform its intended job, add a timer, humidistat or sensor to the fan switch to keep the fan running for at least 20 minutes. The objective is to completely rid the room of moisture.

Never vent the moisture-laden air from the bath or laundry to the attic. This practice sets up a potential disaster for the roof, because venting to the attic eventually damages the roof's plywood sheathing. Typically, it causes decay and rot, which shortens the life of the roof.

Appliances

As discussed earlier, front-loading washing machine release less humidity and use less water than top-loading machines. Dishwasher models also differ in how much humidity they release into the home. When you are preparing to purchase one of these appliances, check its specifications sheet to help guide your selection process. In recent years the EPA has updated its ENERGY STAR requirements for appliances. For more information on ENERGY STAR requirements visit their Web site at http://www.energystar.gov/.

Radon

Radon is a naturally occurring, odorless, colorless gas that is produced in the ground by the radioactive decay of uranium. Although trace amounts of radon exist in all soil from uranium deposits that were raised closer to the Earth's surface or even exposed during glacial periods, variations in ancient glacial activity mean that radon is a greater problem in some areas than in others. It is impossible to predict who might be most at risk; therefore, at the very least every home should be checked for the presence and level of radon.

Radon can affect humans differently according to level and length of exposure. If these radioactively charged alpha particles enter the house and its occupants inhale them, they can embed in lung tissue and cause cellular damage that leads to the development of lung cancer. Recent U.S. studies have documented the relationship between residential radon and lung cancer and shown that radon is the second leading cause of lung cancer in the U.S.

Interestingly, under most circumstances very little radon leaves the ground. Typically, soil radon levels are much higher than concentrations measured in outdoor air. However, a problem may arise in home construction because air tends to rise inside the house and it tends to draw radon from the ground, up through the house, and out the attic vents.

If the average indoor radon level is 4.0 picocuries per liter (pCI/L) or higher, the EPA recommends taking action to mitigate these radon levels. In the U.S., the nationwide indoor radon level averages about 1.3 pCi/L—well below the EPA's limit, but enough to indicate that residential radon testing and mitigation are important aspects of ensuring good indoor air quality.

Even at lower, "acceptable" levels of radon concentration, the longer a person is exposed, the greater the potential impact on his or her health. Longer exposure to a low dose of such radiation can more adversely affect a person's health than a higher dose for a shorter amount of time. Therefore, Belcher Homes installs a passive radon mitigation system in the homes we build (fig. 29).

Here's how it works:

1. We run a 4 in. vertical pipe through a hole in the basement floor into the crushed rock underneath the basement floor slab, creating a siphoning point. We use a "tee" in the gravel and insert about 12 in. of 4 in. drain tile pipe in each end to increase surface area.
2. Next, we seal the pipe in the hole and seal the surface of the floor.

Figure 29. Radon mitigation system

This system takes advantage of the natural stack effect. A siphoning point in the ground under the house vents radon gas to the outside, preventing the house from drawing the radon indoors.

3. Finally, we route the pipe up through the house to an exterior vent in the attic above the eave line.

As the pipe passes through the attic, the warmer air in the attic draws the cooler air from under the slab up through the pipe, mitigating any potential radon hazard in the house. This method also vents moisture-laden air, which keeps the basement drier. As part of our sustainability planning, Belcher Homes tries to keep a 3 ft. vertical run above the attic insulation to accommodate a future fan, if needed.

Chlorine-Reducing Showerheads

Most people are not thinking about chlorine exposure while they shower. However in cities and other urban areas where chlorination is used to help purify water, this type of pollutant can present a health problem. As water sprays through the standard showerhead, the chlorine is vaporized and with every breath you take, you inhale the vapor. The potential impact on human health varies, based on time and exposure as well as other factors. The problem of concentrated chlorine vapor is particularly acute in glass shower enclosures, because they are more airtight, and if you are like my daughters and take 45 minute showers, you could be at greater risk! This risk is lessened with shower curtains.

To mitigate chlorine vaporization, which is a must for asthma sufferers, chlorine-reducing showerheads are now available. Whenever we build homes that are on a municipal water supply (where chlorine is added to the water, unlike homes we build that are served by wells), we recommend to our customers that these chlorine reducing heads be installed. It is just part of the overall promotion of healthier indoor air quality for them.

Green Cleaning Methods

Before presenting a home to its new owners, Belcher Homes has the house thoroughly and meticulously cleaned by professional companies that specialize in using only green cleaning products.

We understand that our cleaning choices affect our health, the livability of our homes, and the health of our planet. Therefore, we choose cleaning products that are formulated to leave the smallest footprint possible on the environment, while effectively cleaning and deodorizing.

According to greenfacts.org, indoor chemicals are in all indoor environments. The extensive use of cleaning agents may influence respiratory health. The products we use to clean a Belcher Home do not contain harmful acids or caustic chemicals. These products will have no negative impact on water resources or on plants and wildlife. They do not contain artificial fragrances, which can aggravate allergies and other chemical sensitivities.

When we worked with the Englemohrs to build their LEED platinum home (figs. 30, 31), they were interested in building green primarily because of their young children. Healthy indoor air quality was of utmost importance (as it should always be when constructing green homes). After incorporating our moisture control process with the materials we used to construct their home and using non-toxic glues, caulks, sealants, paints, and finishes, the last important step was to assure that the products used in the final

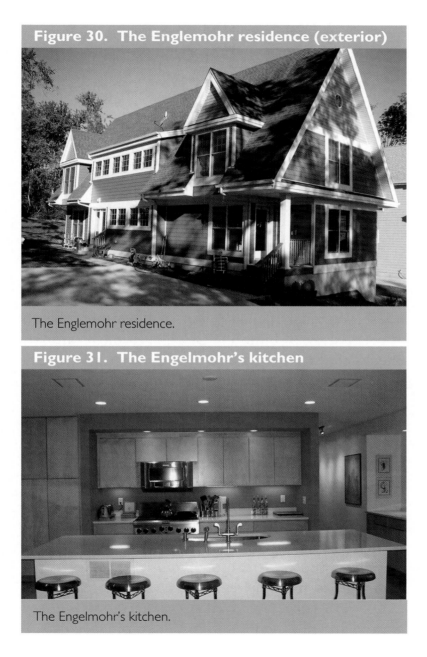

Figure 30. The Englemohr residence (exterior)

The Englemohr residence.

Figure 31. The Engelmohr's kitchen

The Engelmohr's kitchen.

cleaning process would not compromise the indoor air quality we planned for throughout the home's design and construction.

We hire a cleaning company that specializes in using products and techniques that preserve good indoor air quality. According to Mrs. Englemohr, the annual doctor visits for the children dropped dramatically during the past two years. Compared with the previous four years, they dropped from between five and seven visits to one visit.

Managing Moisture

To promote the long-term health and livability of a house, you must manage potential moisture problems at every stage of building. Belcher Homes routinely checks the moisture content of lumber in the sub-flooring, sheathing, and wall framing prior to insulating or covering (fig. 32). If we detect moisture, we use fan heaters to dry out the areas before we proceed with construction. We then cover the areas to prevent moisture from seeping in. This may seem inconsequential, but overlooking it can have dire consequences, such as warping of hardwood flooring or trapping mold-promoting moisture in cavities.

We also insulate all pipes to prevent condensation from creating moisture problems. We never route water pipes in exterior walls because of seasonal temperature differences. Also, condensation is less of a problem with the PEX plumbing piping we use.

Figure 32. Moisture meter

We use a moisture meter like this one to detect moisture in lumber.

All components of a green house must work together to create a healthy indoor environment. Moisture management is critical to the health of your home.

CHAPTER 7

LEARNING TO LIVE GREEN

The leading green home builders do not turn a home buyer loose in a new high-performance green house and hope for the best. Instead, they offer guidance, tips, and detailed information for getting the most out of a highly efficient, sustainable house.

The whole concept of giving a buyer this sort of extra attention and care revolves around the fact that a green house is the high-performance version of the traditional (that is, non-green) house. I liken the difference between the two to buying a Ferrari instead of a Chevy. If I buy a Chevy, I get the keys and a thank-you, whereas if I buy a Ferrari, a technician will show me how to operate and maintain the car in a way that enhances and takes advantage of the car's design and purpose, which is high performance. (Not that I have actually purchased a Ferrari!).

Unlike my automotive example, a green house does not have the price markup compared to a non-green house; in fact, green homes can be very competitively priced, and save their owners money in the long run, because they are less expensive to operate and maintain.

The first thing Belcher Homes does after a home is completed is to invite the customer on a guided tour of their finished home. During our walk-through, we review the home's features together to ensure that customer satisfaction. We explain our philosophy and ideas about green housing and a green lifestyle. We show them how to make their home operate at peak efficiency, just as it has been designed to, and how to adjust all controls, such as the thermostat, for each system. We also make sure they understand how to operate and maintain all appliances.

When we explain passive solar orientation to our customers, we describe how they can take advantage of it to help heat and cool their house throughout the year. We discuss how good landscaping can shade the house in summer, considerably reducing air-conditioning bills, yet allow the house to benefit from direct sunlight during the winter.

We point out the many their home has been designed and built to be sustainable. For example, solar prewiring (solar synapse) will make it easy for the new owners to install solar panels to harvest sunlight and generate electricity on-site for their household, if they ever choose to do so.

One of the most important things Belcher Homes does in terms of customer care is to present each home buyer with an owner's manual, a binder with all the pertinent information specific to their new home. The manual includes the following information:

- warranty and maintenance information for all applicable systems, components, and appliances
- floor plan of the house, showing outlets, valves, and other pertinent operating features
- green building certificate for the home (proof that it passed the verification procedure) and a list of the green building guidelines used to construct the house
- contact information for the suppliers and vendors of every major house system and component
- sources of green furniture and cleaning supplies, green landscapers, and other vendors of relevant products and services
- lists of useful online resources as follows supplemented by print information, such as brochures about building a rain garden:

- the local botanical gardens, so the home owner can find out more about the care and feeding of the native plants around their house
- conservation departments, for information on maintaining wildlife habitats on their property
- educational sites, for information on green housing
- information from local waste management firms on recycling centers for various types of materials, so the home owner will be able to easily recycle items
- information about public transportation, local parks and other community services, as well as brochures and information from the local Chamber of Commerce and local government offices
- tips for saving water, electricity and other natural resources; descriptions of how to use organic pesticides and herbicides properly; composting information; and other green tips
- photos of the home during construction

A Belcher Homes house is not your typical home. We take great pride in that fact and constructing what we think are the best green homes on the market, and we want to help every one of our customers take advantage of their new high-efficiency home. Our customized owner's manual plays an important role in helping us achieve that goal.

We are constantly encouraged by the tremendous customer buy-in to living a greener lifestyle. Most, if not all, consumers genuinely pay attention to their utility bills and recycling efforts. Once they see the change in their cost to live in a green home compared with their previous homes, they continually look for ways to keep lowering their utility bills. Most home owners track their energy usage, which is key to increasing energy efficiency. I always enjoy experiencing the enthusiasm of our customers. A builder could not ask for a better sales team than these satisfied home owners.

Figures 33 and 34 show charts provided by a Belcher Homes customer comparing the actual cost of living in their new home to their previous century home and the probable costs for two other types of homes.

The Pedersens are empty nesters, who moved from a villa home. They liked their previous home's floor plan, but preferred to have a single family home. Their new green ranch home has the same dimensions as their previous villa home. Therefore, as the Pedersen's track their utility bills they are comparing apples to apples. Their utility bills are 45% less, on average, than their villa unit. Mr. Pedersen actually compiled his own brochure to show guests and the occasional drive by stranger who is interested in green homes. Talk about a great sales person!

Figure 33. Home comparison chart
Results
Average Monthly utility costs, 4 bedrooms, 2600 s.f:

House Type	Typical Non-Green House	Green House As designed	Green House Actual	Existing House (100+ yrs old)
Gas $/MO rate: $0.86/therm	**$90.73** 105.5 Therms	**$54.46** 63.33 Therm	**$51.58** 59.98 Therms	**$130.04** 154.7 Therms
Electric Rate: $0.065/kwh	**$68.40** 1052.36 kWh	**$41.04** 631.42 kWh	**$64.17** 987.22 kWh	**$144.92** 2229.50 kWh
Total Monthly Utility Cost	**$159.13** *Baseline*	**$95.50** *41% better*	**$115.75** *29% better*	**$274.96** **72% worse**

Heating=68 degrees
Cooling=78 degrees   ** note: prices do not include city taxes and service fees*

The first column shows the average home of typical construction. The second column shows their new home if built with everything on their "wish list." The third column reflects their home as actually constructed, and the fourth column reflects the smaller, older home they moved from. The results speak for themselves!

The Engelmohr's and Pedersens are just two examples of the great relationships that develop when you build a high-quality green home. Our customers see us as their advocates when building green. We try hard to stay abreast of new technologies and diligent about what we incorporate into our homes to make sure we are the best advocates we can be.

Figure 34. The waste diet
Living a sustainable lifestyle.

 Construction waste was **60%** less than conventional construction.

 Engelmohr household landfill waste is **85%** less than the average household waste.

Monthly household landfill waste	Average Household 4 People	Engelmohr Household 4 People
Jan 2008	240 lbs	23 lbs
Feb 2008	240 lbs	27 lbs
Mar 2008	240 lbs	44 lbs
Apr 2008	240 lbs	57 lbs
May 2008	240 lbs	49 lbs
June 2008	240lbs	17 lbs *(to date)*
Total	1440 lbs	217 lbs

The Engelmohr's participated in a program called "The Waste Diet." Not only were we available to reduce construction waste during construction of their home, the Engelmohr's took it a step further. As you can see they are really making a statement!

CHAPTER 8

GREEN CHOICES HAVE GLOBAL IMPACT

As home builders, we must never lose sight of the fact that what we do has a global impact. Our personal and business choices have worldwide political, social, and environmental consequences. The actions of each person ripple outward to touch the lives of many people and affect the natural world.

Choosing to build a green home or renovating, retrofitting, or remodeling an older home to be more green allows builders to play a constructive role in improving the quality of life for everyone. Even small changes, such as installing low-flow toilets in an older home, add up. We can all take steps toward living more green lives.

Creating a Plus-Plus

No- and low-VOC paints, sealants, and flooring help create better indoor air quality, which affects your customers' health in positive ways (fig. 35). On a global scale, scientists say the elements that compose VOCs harm the ozone layer and that, by comparison, VOC-free finishes and materials leave a softer footprint on the world. That's a plus for future generations. Our

Figure 35. Hard surfaces in kitchen

This kitchen features hard surfaces including cabinetry with low-voc finishes, white oak hardwood floors, and a direct vent fireplace.

choices can have a positive or a negative multiplier effect. When Belcher Homes installs carpeting, for example, we select only formaldehyde and toxin-free products. We know it is better for our customers' health, as well as the health and sustainability of our planet.

Green builders use readily recyclable materials—that is, no- and low-VOC materials—when constructing a new house, and use materials that add durability, which enhances a home's livability and extends its lifespan. Because many of these materials also can be recycled easily, every component in the house eventually can be reclaimed and reused to make something new, lessening the impact of the house on the Earth and its natural resources. Recycling construction materials and entire houses saves energy in the manufacturing process as well as natural resources and landfill space.

Native landscaping is another opportunity for builders to improve our world. You can add landscaping that the home owner does not have to water as often in the summer, because the plants are so adapted to their climate and soil they can fend for themselves. Select decorative, ornamental, native plants that are perfectly suited to your area, and you will save home owners from maintenance while conserving our precious water resources. The local water treatment plant won't have to purify as much water; with less demand for water, the plant won't need to expand. The net result is that everyone saves energy, money, and natural resources.

Using native plants also helps save our natural forests, meadows, and wetlands from being overtaken by aggressive, invasive nonnative species as well. For example, Japanese honeysuckle is rampant in the Midwest. It chokes out native vines wherever it grows. Kudzu has been called "the plant that ate the South." Purple Loosestrife (not to be confused with other native Loosestrife species) was introduced into wetlands has now become an aggressive pest. I'm sure you know of many other examples in your own area.

The *National Green Building Standard* credits builders and developers for incorporating good landscape practices including eradication of these invasive species and replacing with noninvasive, native plants.

The problem with many cultivated garden species is that they depend on rich soils, frequent watering, and other high-maintenance routines simply to live, grow, and bloom at their peak. Expect to spend a lot of money on mulch, fertilizer, soil amendments, and other techniques if you want to coax nonnative cultivars to grow in your community.

Native species not only use less water, they require little if any fertilizer, herbicide, insecticide, mulch, soil amendments, etc. Using native species also helps to preserve and promote local ecosystems, so your corner of the universe will not only be healthier, it will retain its individual character. Think of the global impact if every builder chose to include native plants in their landscaping designs.

Ensuring Watershed Health

Watershed health starts at the home site and extends to aquifers, lakes, rivers, streams and eventually to the ocean. What we do on the home front has a pretty impressive impact on natural water resources. We typically try to think of our home sites as giant catcher's mitts for rainfall. Overall, water is a builder's worst enemy. Therefore, we try to minimize its impact on the home and divert it as quickly as possible. We know water will run off roofs and hardscapes, such as walks and driveways, along with falling on other areas of the site.

If we can incorporate landscape features, or swales, to capture or at least slow the water down so that it can be absorbed into the ground or evaporate, and minimize the amount of hardscapes, it can have positive impacts on storm water runoff and overall watershed quality. There are tremendous resources available to help with plant selection and overall design for rain gardens and bioswales.

We developed and built in the Labarque Creek Watershed site before we knew it was the last clean watershed in the St. Louis, Missouri, area. However, when we found out, through our practices and focus in building to the National Green Building Guidelines, we knew we had not damaged it. I guess you could say we did the right thing without even trying; we certainly outsmarted ourselves.

Our customer had already purchased a lot in this development. The guidelines helped us determine where to place the home on the lot and how to manage the natural resources on and around the home site. Our practices of identifying clearing limits and hand clearing wooded home sites really paid off. It cost us about 20% less to clear sites this way and mitigated possible damage to trees, other foliage, and grades from machinery due to steepness and other site conditions. It also lent itself to minimizing storm water problems during clearing because the ground cover is not disturbed until we actually remove topsoil and excavate the foundation.

As discussed earlier, we typically engage an arborist to determine the viability of trees we want to remove as well as those we want to protect. Money we save in clearing land will easily pay for the arborist.

Old-Growth Wood

Belcher Homes strives to use sustainably grown and harvested lumber. We do this because we want to ensure our forests are sustainable and will be able to support wildlife habitat and natural ecosystems for generations to come. The sustainability of our industry depends on sustainable forest management.

The timber industry has begun to take serious steps toward sustainable forest management. Most wood today comes from tree farms or second-growth forests, which are almost all managed to maintain the forests' ecosystems. For example, there are stringent rules and regulations for how companies may harvest timber, including how to cross a creek or build a road, and how to take timber out.

Moreover, new materials and construction designs can use wood fiber more productively, effectively reducing the amount of sustainable lumber required to build a house. Engineered lumber, synthetic hardwoods, ingenious methods of reusing waste wood, and wood-saving designs make efficient use of wood, cutting total costs while yielding strength, durability and stability.

Old-growth forests provide enormous benefits for the health and livability of our planet. They support fish, wildlife and, indirectly, people. These forests help conserve biodiversity and water resources, and create places of great beauty. These forests also help clean the air and sequester carbon, thereby reducing the effect of greenhouse gases.

Although sustainably managing these forests, including harvesting old-growth trees to benefit an entire forest is essential, unfortunately, the financial and environmental costs to harvest lumber in these forests, often may exceed the market value of the lumber they contain. We all want to protect these forests, which are a terrific heritage, and obtain our lumber from tree farms and well-managed forests instead.

Proper management of the world's forest resources must take into account short-term and long-term environmental and social values.

Energy Efficiency

By increasing energy efficiency, we can build fewer power-generating facilities. Smarter use of energy reduces the demand for minerals and oil, allowing us to avoid mining and drilling, which deplete the Earth of nonrenewable resources. In addition, the potential capital investment in such projects can be reallocated to more productive uses.

Energy conservation is the "first fuel" when it comes to meeting America's (and the world's) demand for energy.

As we search for renewable energy technologies, conservation is the greenest approach, and efficiency is the smartest approach. They remain the most cost-effective and reliable methods available for getting the most out of every unit of energy. The marketplace is starting to validate green and efficient technology.

For example, Austin, Texas, used to have higher utility rates than it does now. Today the city enjoys some of the lowest utility rates, even with steady population growth. There's no magic to it and it's not a fluke. The plain fact is that the people of Austin decided to focus on energy conservation. They also decided to build more energy-efficient housing and office buildings. In 1991, they instituted one of the first green building programs in the country. Energy conservation that lowered demand for power opened the door to lower utility rates. If Austin did it, why can't other cities and towns? What about your community? Viable green building program models are out there; all they need is a little promotion.

A promising path to rapidly and exponentially increase overall energy conservation would be retrofitting older homes. In the U.S. alone, about 98% of existing homes were built with components and technology more than 20 years old. If we updated their building envelopes, windows, appliances, HVAC, plumbing, and insulation following green guidelines, we could cut their use of energy and water by up to 40% or more in some areas. The economics, as well as the energy policy, are sound.

Recently a lot of attention has been focused on ratcheting up building codes and government regulations to require even tighter constraints on the home building industry in new home construction. While the industry has taken great strides to improve building performance and accelerated these efforts by incorporating green building techniques, new regulations inevitably drive new home costs up, which will prevent many consumers from moving out of older and substantially less efficient homes and into new green homes.

As an old, recycled code official, I know that newer homes are inherently better and safer than older homes. However, the cost of unnecessary additional regulations inhibits people's ability to afford to move from their older, less efficient homes.

Climate change and global warming are receiving a tremendous amount of attention. There are proposed changes that would eliminate some of the climate specific issues that the green building guidelines take into account. One example is the proposed rule requiring *cool roofs* in colder climate areas. Cool roofs could and most likely would, be less energy efficient in these areas as it would take more energy to heat these buildings.

Policy makers typically focus on the high-profile topic of energy in discussions about green building. However, the *National Green Building Standard* and USGBC's LEED-H all encompass much more than energy efficiency. Wise, high-efficient use of all natural resources and home design must not be overshadowed by one specific concern or issue. The fact is, green building programs now exist and will accomplish the energy and conservation goals that policy makers, and all of us, want. They simply need to be enabled and promoted, and consumers and builders must be educated about their use and application.

It is said that charity begins at home—so does the global impact of building green. It benefits you and your children, and will benefit your grandchildren, your community, and the Earth. It is not just how we leave the world for future generations; the sustainability of our industry is also at stake. It's a profession and an industry I have committed myself to far more than I imagined I would when I started out. That's why I build green.

INDEX